ADVANCE PRAISE

"Ram is among the world's top business thinkers. Many of the world's best CEOs have benefitted from Ram's wisdom. As we enter this era of lurching change, please read Ram's insights on leading through inflation to reinvent your own approach to this contemporary challenge."

—FRED HASSAN, DIRECTOR, WARBURG PINCUS

"A must-read book for today's CXOs—since most have never had experience delivering results in high inflation environments. Drawing on learnings from their multi-decade experience and from extensive research into the current business world, Ram and Geri clearly articulate 2nd and 3rd order impacts of inflation (beyond the obvious cost-price relationship) and offer empirically proven and practical solutions that are useful to businesses in all industries."

—RAJ RATNAKAR, SENIOR VICE PRESIDENT AND CHIEF STRATEGY OFFICER, DUPONT

"Some sound, valuable and timely insights from Charan and his partner on how to effectively deal with current and potentially insidious effects of inflation. A necessary read led by a renowned savvy veteran."

—LARRY BOSSIDY, FORMER CHAIR AND CEO OF HONEYWELL, COAUTHOR OF BESTSELLER *EXECUTION*

"Ram Charan, one of the smartest people out there today, delivers a level of insight and wisdom that can be found nowhere else. The lessons he offers are exceptional. If success is a goal for you, read this book and then share it with your closest friend."

—BOB DILENSCHNEIDER, CHAIRMAN AND CEO, THE DILENSCHNEIDER GROUP

"Ram's must-do actions to outpace inflation for business managers, functional leaders, and board members are mission critical in our resource-constrained world."

—CHAD HOLLIDAY, CO-CHAIR, MISSION POSSIBLE PARTNERSHIP

LEADING THROUGH INFLATION

Other Books by Ram Charan

LEADING THROUGH INFLATION

AND RECESSION
AND STAGFLATION

RAM CHARAN
AND GERI WILLIGAN

IDEAPRESS
PUBLISHING

WASHINGTON, D.C.

IDEAPRESS
PUBLISHING

Published in the United States by Ideapress Publishing.

Ideapress Publishing | www.ideapress.com

All trademarks are the property of their respective companies.

Cover Design: Pete Garceau
Interior Design: Jessica Angerstein

Cataloging-in-Publication Data is on file with the Library of Congress.

ISBN: 978-1-64687-121-6

Special Sales
Ideapress Books are available at a special discount for bulk purchases for sales promotions and premiums, or for use in corporate training programs. Special editions, including personalized covers, a custom foreword, corporate imprints, and bonus content, are also available.

2 3 4 5 6 7 8 9 10

Dedicated to the hearts and souls of the joint family
of twelve siblings and cousins living under one roof
for fifty years, whose personal sacrifices made
my formal education possible.

—Ram Charan

CONTENTS

The Urgency
To Act

This book began when the world stepped into an economic era not seen for some 40 years. In the first half of 2022, people were grappling with high inflation and starting to talk about the possibility of recession and stagflation. Things were getting tough.

But when the going gets tough, the tough get going. Some of the business leaders I saw responding to inflation reminded me of the people I knew at General Electric Company in the early 1980s, when a similar bout of inflation took hold. Then-CEO Jack Welch asked me to conduct a program for executives across the company, which we called COIN, for Coping with Inflation. Those leaders learned about inflation's insidious effects, took the lessons back to the businesses they ran, and helped GE come through that period in great shape.

It is in that spirit of providing practical guidance that Geri and I coauthored this book. It has hands-on advice for what to do, how to do it, when to do it, and how to anticipate what is coming ahead. These ideas have been tested in practice and are useful to people in every part of the organization.

If there is one overarching message it is to move quickly, because the economic damage comes fast. This book is designed to speed your learning and to shorten the time for you to act.

—RAM CHARAN

CHAPTER 1

What You Need To Know About Inflation

We now live in an environment of ugly inflation and a looming recession. Rising costs, persistent shortages, and pricing that is often behind the curve pose a whole new challenge to business leaders, most of whom have never managed through a period like this.

It is your job as a leader to steer the company through inflation, whether or not you have practice at it. That means fully understanding how inflation touches every part of the business and enlisting the help of others in the company to combat it. Hunkering down until the Federal Reserve fixes things is not a viable plan.

Think of the economic shift as a chance to reset the business, and learn from other leaders who are showing a realistic, actionable path to thrive in the new economic context. Some business leaders have moved swiftly, even preemptively, to stem potential damage to the business from shrinking margins, shaky volume, and cash shortages. Some saw inflation coming and raised prices early on, sometimes by as much as 20%. Chanel raised prices on some of its luxury goods three times in 2021.

The early movers are taking steps to weather the current economic conditions and, more than that, strengthening the business for what will unfold on the other side of inflation and recession some three or four years down the road. They are showing tremendous optimism in accepting the new realities and rethinking the basics of their business—from its compensation plan and pricing strategy to its mix of customers and business model.

This book lays out the hazards of inflation and how to avoid them so your company will survive this difficult time. It will help you build your confidence to act decisively despite the unknowns by showing how other leaders are stemming the damage and resetting their businesses for a brighter future. It will help you see inflation's impact through a wider lens and give you specific tools for dealing with it, including simple things like bringing people together from across the organization to address the challenges the new economic context presents. All of those tools and approaches will prepare you to contend with recession or stagflation if and when they come.

THE UNIVERSAL TRUTHS ABOUT INFLATION

You don't need charts and graphs to know that costs have been rising. But there's more to know about how inflation affects a business. You need to understand what inflation does to a company, an industry, and the economy as whole.

Here are some important facts about inflation that may not be obvious until it is too late:

1. **Inflation consumes cash.** Cash gets trapped in inventories and accounts receivable for the same unit volume. Growth gobbles up even more cash.

2. **Price increases roll through the value chain to the end consumer like a freight train, disrupting the economics and power balance of players along the way.** At some point, consumers will push back and demand drops.

3. **Aggregate measures like the Consumer Price Index don't tell you much about how inflation will affect your company.** Microsegmentation across your business and the supply chain is essential.

4. **The effects of inflation are cumulative.** A 7% inflation rate may be manageable for one year but a rate even close to that compounded over several years could ravage the business.

5. **Inflation trends are partly psychological.** When people expect continual price increases, they hoard goods, creating even more demand and exacerbating the imbalance. This pattern can lead to hyper-inflation.

6. **Inflation can turn well-planned capital expenditures into bad investments.** Earlier decisions were likely based on assumptions that are no longer valid.

7. **Sacrificing customer trust to protect the business from higher costs has long-term consequences.** It is hard to restore a brand once it is tarnished.

8. **Inflation reorders competition.** It is an opportunity for businesses that can sustain in the near term and strengthen their position for future growth.

These truths show why many business leaders need a broader and more urgent response to inflation than they have undertaken thus far. They should help you appreciate that the kind of cost cutting many companies have been doing to struggle through the immediate hardships will not get them through a sustained period of inflation above, say, 7%, let alone a spurt of hyper-inflation, recession, or stagflation.

THE BRIGHT SIDE
OF INFLATION

The current disruption to your company may make it hard to appreciate the eighth universal truth about inflation: it creates opportunities to improve your competitive position. But dealing with inflation's negative impact on the business will reveal a silver lining.

For one thing, some of the excesses that were tolerated in a zero-cost-of-capital environment will be squeezed out. The business will sharpen its focus and cultivate a stronger set of customers. You'll find ways to improve productivity and cut costs through more automation, or use technology to serve customers better with less cash usage. You may be a smaller company in the interim, but the cash you conserve or withdraw from projects that are no longer winners can be used to create new products, or even a new industry.

Look four years down the road and prepare to take advantage of the post-inflation world. The economy will have changed, and your industry and business model might well have changed too. New companies may have entered your space, because technological advancement doesn't stop. What will make you better prepared?

The company's response to inflation will be a differentiator, along the lines of ESG. Inflation will hurt those who can't manage their cash right, because the demand for cash—and therefore any shortage—is compounding. That creates an opportunity for you to lead an industry consolidation or to acquire critical talent, technology, or patents.

Your psychology will make a difference. Play offense. Take inflation seriously, adapt faster, and bring the rest of the organization with you.

WHY EVERYONE NEEDS TO KNOW ABOUT INFLATION

The most common effect of inflation is rising costs, something your company is probably already experiencing. In an effort to protect margins, it's tempting for a CEO to turn to the people who manage the supply chain. Ram's recent visit with a large consumer-goods company is a case in point. When the cost of raw materials started to increase sharply in early 2022, the CEO called a meeting to discuss the problem. He assumed his usual hands-off management style: he delegated the task of recouping those increased costs to the supply chain.

Left on their own, there was only so much those people could do. Other business functions didn't sense any urgency to consider their role in combatting inflation. For people in sales and marketing, for example, it was basically business as usual, with little adjustment in pricing or the number of SKUs (stock keeping units).

What that company and many others are missing is that inflation affects nearly every part of the business. That's why the entire organization must confront it. Why do sales and marketing have to be involved? Because inflation consumes cash. Every unit sold ties up more cash in inventory. If customers extend their payments, as they may have already started to do, accounts receivable will consume more cash too.

Meanwhile, if the sales force is reluctant to increase prices, or to increase them enough, margins and cash suffer. It may be uncomfortable for those on the front line, and even for the CEO, who wonders what will happen if they increase prices. Will competitors follow? Will customers be upset and market share crumble?

A study of 344 U.S. CEOs of industrial businesses by consulting firm Simon-Kucher & Partners found that as of March 2022, one-third of those businesses had not made any price increases for inflation. Price increases that lag behind cost increases cause margins to contract and, worse, can lead to insolvency.

Finance has to be involved to manage cash and, along with HR, to revise performance metrics. In this new economic environment, the usual performance metrics can become downright dangerous—that is, compensation incentives that push for revenue growth and market-share gains without consideration of cash consumption can bring the company to the brink. Growth projections and payback periods can be deeply distorted as well, particularly if the gap between your cost increases and pricing is not properly addressed.

Leaders have to change their priorities. Many have been in hot pursuit of revenue growth and market-share gains throughout their career. Now they may need an abrupt shift to become a smaller, financially sturdy business. They have to focus on the balance sheet, especially cash, and get the entire organization on the same page. Communication with employees is critical, as is keeping investors informed.

FROM CONFUSION TO CONTROL

We can all agree that the era of near-zero interest rates and ultra-low inflation is far behind us. Some saw the change coming sooner than others and took action accordingly. But spikes in energy and food costs from the Russo-Ukrainian War, along with prolonged shortages in supplies from COVID-19 and extended Chinese shutdowns, have created their own kind of chaos. Many leaders are feeling unprepared. Their confidence has been nicked.

This is a time to play offense, to lead with discipline, and move proactively. Every delayed price increase has an enduring impact on the business. Every day that cash is not collected from delinquent customers is a step closer to financial distress. In high inflation, timing clearly matters.

The shift from low to high inflation calls on you to learn some new management tools to deal with it. This book is organized to provide them. It describes best practices of companies that have been adapting quickly to the new environment with the specificity that makes those practices replicable. You will learn to read the **early warning signs** of economic shifts, so you can be preemptive versus reactive; manage for **cash,** avoiding cash traps and ensuring liquidity; be smart on **pricing**, knowing what approach to use where and its timing; evaluate the **value chain** for opportunities to protect cash and margins; and use inflation as a chance to reset the **business model**. The final chapter walks you through specific issues **each business function** should address.

Along the way, it will show how leaders have converted from a "grow grow grow!" mentality to one focused on a smaller, higher quality company; reined in costly programs without sacrificing the future; managed talent in a rising-wage environment; and kept ecosystem and customer relationships intact.

The economy is nowhere near settled, and no one can see into the future, but decisions must be made and resources committed on a daily basis. This is a call for leaders to step up to the new game.

CHAPTER 2

A War Room To Pick Up Early Warning Signals

Inflation intensified in late 2021. Then came Russia's invasion of Ukraine, followed by sanctions, and China's lockdown of entire cities due to COVID-19, which kicked shortages and prices into overdrive. Some cost increases may have been predictable, but the sudden constriction of Russian oil and Ukrainian agricultural products was a shock.

Companies that have a mechanism to detect such changes and coordinate a response sooner are better positioned than others. It's how Catalent, a contract development and manufacturing organization to the biopharma industry, has been able to adjust to rising wage costs and prepare for a host of potential disruptions to its value chain. As CEO John Chiminski puts it, "It's a situation where you need to at least be riding the curve and not be behind the curve."

As early as June 2021, Chiminski and his team were convinced that the wage inflation Catalent was experiencing would not go away. "There was a lot coming out in the news around that time saying that the inflation numbers were transitory," Chiminski told us, "but as we saw things unfolding, we came to a different conclusion.

"There was a shortage of workers in general, and in our very specific high-demand biopharma space, it was even more acute. In specific geographic areas, namely Boston, San Diego, Baltimore, San Francisco, and North Carolina, which are kind of the hubs of biopharma in the United States, you had almost hyper wage growth combined with a significant increase in turnover. As a company, our turnover rate had consistently been around 9% through the pandemic. It jumped to 11% in 2021, and then in the first part of 2022 to 13%. That nearly doubled our EOP."

The very name Catalent is a combination of Catalyst and Talent, signifying that gifted, knowledge workers are at the heart of the company's value creation. Keeping up with market wages was non-negotiable. How could they sustain the business while paying what was necessary to attract talent? Chiminski and his team commenced those discussions immediately, and their urgency only increased as raw-material costs began to rise steeply as well.

This is what war rooms are for. Whether or not you use the term, every company needs a mechanism to get people's attention focused on the urgent threat from high inflation and to enlist their help in executing a solution. Some companies have simply changed the content of existing meeting formats. Others have created something new.

Best practice is not just to examine the immediate threats to the business but to look ahead and make judgments about what might be coming next, an exercise of gathering data and reasoning out the possibilities. An ideal war room is not just for firefighting; it is also strategic. Early warning signals will tell you not just where the problems are emerging but also their pace. They allow you to be predictive, prescriptive, and preemptive.

If the CEO doesn't take the initiative to create a war room, the board should propose it. Maybe do an off-site with the top team. Conversely, the CEO may want to call a special meeting of the board solely to discuss how inflation and recession will affect the company. If you're a leader and don't see why you need such things, skip ahead to the chapters on cash and pricing, and you will be convinced that you do.

EVERY COMPANY NEEDS A WAR ROOM

A war room is a frequent gathering of people (face-to-face or not) who will aggregate information, strategize, and drive the plan. It has an important social purpose in aligning and intensifying people's focus. Much as in a military situation, it is an excellent way to convert anxiety and fear into energy and action.

By now, inflation is not new to you. But the anxiety and fear it has stirred have likely taken root. When otherwise confident business leaders are unsure how to deal with it, reactions slow. Delays can mean shrinking margins and dwindling cash, and once you fall behind in pricing it is hard to catch up.

One way to get people's attention is with a meeting of the entire C-suite to learn from outsiders how inflation affected businesses in the past and how they responded, especially in the 1970s in the U.S. and in the 1980s and 1990s in Brazil. At one point, Brazilians were rushing to buy food in the morning because supermarkets increased prices during the day, something Ram witnessed when he was teaching there.

Move quickly to focus on your business by establishing a cadence of meetings at least once a week, but probably more often. Some manufacturing companies have daily meetings of the CEO, COO, and heads of manufacturing and purchasing.

In late 2021, the top team at Catalent started meeting at least weekly, in addition to launching a companywide Total Cost Excellence initiative. Chiminski laid out the dilemma in blunt terms: "We can't stop wages and costs from increasing, and we have to be competitive in the markets where we participate. That means we have to take significant costs out of our business. In addition to that, we need to rebuild the muscle of price increases." As the meetings continued, discussion of what was happening quickly evolved into specific steps and assignments.

Soon after Ed Breen took the helm as CEO of DuPont in 2020, just prior to COVID setting in, he established a one-hour weekly meeting of the company's top 10 or so leaders. Throughout COVID they joined by video conference every Monday morning, typically to focus on operational issues. It was an effective tool for running the company in ordinary times, and it became even more useful when the unexpected arose. When the COVID-19 pandemic broke out, Breen, an experienced CEO who had already managed through several crises, brought out his playbook. He nominated a member of his leadership team as the "COVID czar" and had that person report to the group on what was happening where, how COVID-19 was impacting the work force, and how it was being managed.

In the fall of 2021, as shortages and price increases began to accelerate, the chief procurement officer began to join in to directly brief the corporate leadership team. He brought data and perspectives from experts on things like how much air and ocean freight was rising, what was happening with key raw materials, and where a force majeure was threatening to disrupt the business.

When Russia attacked Ukraine in February 2022, attention was riveted on energy supply and price levels. "The CPO suddenly became a rock star who everybody wanted to talk to," as Raj Ratnakar, senior vice president and chief strategy officer at DuPont, put it. "He and his team were running around gathering metrics, picking up the latest trends, and presenting them to us every other week, and we are all there taking it in and asking questions.

"That information trickles down through the organization, so everybody is on top of it. When we were shown that the cost of natural gas was going up, we immediately tied it back to implications on our raw material and logistics costs. We were able to stay ahead of the curve. We knew we had to raise prices on products that were impacted, like next week! If not, there would be imminent impact on our financial performance."

Energizing people to spring to action based on information others share is valuable, but there's another benefit: it sensitizes everyone to early warning signals they may be exposed to in the normal course of their workday.

WHAT TO LOOK FOR

In early 2022, India's entire textile industry, from growing cotton to clothing manufacturing, was poised to grow as the government passed legislation supporting the industry. A large manufacturer of fiber was gearing up to expand its capacity to meet a planned sales increase in Europe.

But then the early warning signals started flashing. One after another, European textile manufacturers started cancelling orders. Europe was hit hard by the war in Ukraine, which sent its energy prices soaring. Anticipating that high energy costs would constrain consumers' budgets and affect their psychology, clothing manufacturers were pulling back to keep their own businesses afloat. The fiber manufacturer had to scale back too, moving fast to taper its production and exploring an even steeper reduction in capacity, even as competitors in India continued on an expansion path.

Early warning signals can come from your customers, as they did in this case, your supply chain, or from industry statistics. Don't wait until they are obvious. Every company should create a dashboard and put thought into what to include. If you don't have people who can create a dashboard quickly, outsource it. Vendors can get it done in just a few months.

Along with some macroeconomic measures you find useful, choose some metrics that are specific and critical to your business. The CPI is useful for policymakers and headline writers, but it doesn't capture inflation's impact on a particular industry, business, or subsector. Besides, CPI is a trailing indicator. Even the PPI (producer price index, which measures prices paid to producers of goods and services) is ahead of it. In assessing the risk of stagflation in the U.S., respected economist Mohamed El-Erian told Bloomberg co-anchor Jonathan Ferro in a May 13, 2022, interview that the PPI had just risen 11%. El-Erian added, "We haven't quite realized that the PPI numbers are a leading indicator of the CPI numbers. We need to focus on that as well."

Don't get stuck on any single number. Inflation rates will vary sector by sector and subsector by subsector. Granularity will make the difference here. Think about what metrics may be especially relevant to your business. For instance, a heavy manufacturer that consumes a lot of energy tracks the CPI as well as a fuel index.

Digital technology is a great tool for gathering external data. It can scrape the web for publicly available data on pricing and demand and send alerts when price competition is taking place and people are fighting for market share. It's not uncommon for consumer prices to change daily, whereas for industrial companies, at least pre-inflation, prices might change once a month.

Data can help you detect shifts in buying patterns, from which you can draw other inferences. In a May 2022 earnings call, Walmart executives noted a change in the mix of consumer purchases in the recent quarter—a lower proportion of total sales were in the general merchandise category, and within the grocery category there was a shift to more private-label versus branded goods as inflation hit double digits. The shift from general merchandise to groceries affected gross margins, among other things, and inventories and therefore cash—

important information given Walmart's stated concern that inflation would continue to increase.

Be sure you are monitoring internal early warning signals as well. Lack of cash kills companies, so the CEO and CFO should get updates on it regularly to know when inventories are beginning to tick upward and when average days of accounts receivable is lengthening.

REASON OUT WHAT'S COMING NEXT

The only way you can be preemptive—to get ahead of the curve or to at least ride it, as Chiminski says—is to be predictive. That means making judgments that go beyond the facts and data points you collect as early warning signals. Use your war room to brainstorm what the data are pointing to, what trends are emerging, and take some leaps to consider how things could combine to create what's next. The thought process will set you apart.

Posing questions is a great stimulant. Even if the topics seem a bit far afield, they can generate insights that become highly relevant to your business. As you read about the impact of inflation on various countries, you might consider how emerging economies will be affected. Albert Chao, CEO of Westlake Chemical, said, "We are going to see currency and inflation issues in the emerging economies. They will have liquidity issues. What happens for their demand? Could that be an instigator of social unrest? What would be the effects of that?"

As Americans use the financial cushion they got from fiscal-stimulus programs, will demand decline at the same time costs are rising? How would that impact a consumer business?

DK Agarwal, CEO and CFO of Indorama Ventures, considered whether people in Europe would drive fewer miles as energy costs soared. Would they therefore replace their tires less frequently? Indorama Ventures is a global sustainable chemical company based in Thailand that makes a range of products, from resins and PET (polyethylene terephthalate) packaging to technical yarns and fabrics. Also on Indorama Ventures' product list: the cord material used to manufacture tires.

There are plenty of experts dissecting every statement from the Federal Reserve for signals about a slowdown in the U.S. economy. But the Fed doesn't control everything, and you may have your own mix of factors and line of reasoning. What is the lag time between Fed action and a downturn? Whereas some people think recession will come sooner, Agarwal reminds us that inflation came nearly two years after stimulus money was dispersed. If you reach the point where you firmly believe recession will come in late 2023, plan for it now when it is five or six quarters ahead while watching for signs to the contrary.

In your search for "warnings," don't overlook the positives. You can expect that inflation will cause some sectors to grow, such as defense and risk management. What else?

Your questions may be centered on inflation now, but as conditions change, reframe them around the possibility of recession. When will it come, how long will it last, and what will precipitate it and make it last longer?

ACT QUICKLY

Early recognition of rising wages and costs triggered a whole series of actions at Catalent, which you will hear more about in chapter five. For leaders accustomed to stability, it may be hard to overcome analysis paralysis, but the speed of response is now a competitive advantage.

Consider how DuPont benefitted when the top team moved quickly on the CPO's warnings of imminent cost increases. Ratnakar explains, "What's interesting is how people have reacted. On the one hand, we do our best to contain costs by finding every operational lever in our playbook—looking for alternate sources, alternate materials where feasible, buying from alternate regions, switching modes of transportation, etcetera. In parallel, we do not lose time in going after price. If you're not able to cover the cost of your raw materials and all the other COGS [cost of goods sold] increases as well as your logistics increases, you're definitely in a poor position. There's been a more than 200% increase in the cost of certain kinds of freight. The chemical and materials science industry often has dependencies on petrochemicals that are sort of tied back to gas prices."

Ratnakar continues, "I credit our CEO Ed Breen, a wise man with many years of experience, for urging our leadership team to get very proactive and data driven in covering those cost increases with pricing. Our peers have actually been slow to recognize—and even slower to react to—cost increases. Everybody has increased price a little bit, but it's a question of how quickly and how much. If you're not proactive, your P&L is always lagging."

He goes on to explain, "The effect on financial performance is even more acute in market segments where businesses have low operating margins. While companies like DuPont operate at margin levels of about 20%, lots of upstream chemical companies like BASF operate with lower operating margins, often less than 10%. When such companies do not react effectively, or take too long to digest movements in raw material and freight prices and therefore do not react, the impact on profitability can be devastating.

"During normal times, even a 2% or 3% price increase is considered unusual in many of our markets and in the industrial world in general. In electronics, most products actually have negative price changes in normal times. If you're getting 4% growth of the overall business, talking about a 2%

price increase would, in a normal year, be pretty impressive. "That's actually a good, healthy industrial business compared to the industry averages that are often at 1% or less.

"As a result of our effective execution, our earnings have actually been much more resilient compared with our peers, and we've gotten a lot of credit from our investors and analysts for that. It is the timing, as well as the magnitude."

EARLY WARNING SIGNS IN THE ECONOMY

For more than a decade and a good part of many leaders' careers, the economy chugged upward. Uncertainty was mostly around how fast it would grow, not whether it would. CEOs, CFOs, and other leaders are now pressed to become armchair economists with little preparation for that role. Who should they listen to? What metrics should they watch? Ultimately, they need to develop their own set of metrics and experts to listen to, and then, in consultation with their teams, form their own point of view.

No doubt you are already tuned into announcements and innuendo by the Fed. But what else will indicate the pace and magnitude of interest-rate changes? At what point will the Fed's quantitative tightening suppress growth and trigger all the spillover effects that lead to recession or stagflation?

The Federal Reserve has promised to increase interest rates and shrink its balance sheet, both of which will have an impact on mortgage rates and borrowing rates, and therefore on housing, car sales, and credit card volume. In turn, travel and entertainment will be affected. These are normal happenings when the Fed uses its weapons of the balance sheet and interest rates to control inflation. It has begun.

What will prolong inflation is persistently high energy prices that get factored into the prices of seemingly everything. When inflation rears up at every turn, it affects people's psychology. The general public will want hard evidence to believe that inflation is subsiding.

The word **recession** is now in many people's working vocabulary, but the timing and depth are uncertain. Ram's view is that the Fed is preparing to precipitate a recession sooner, while unemployment is low. A recession may well have begun by the time this book is printed. If not, it could well come in early 2023 and last for 18 months or so. Inflation could last longer.

Whatever your estimation of the timing, get ready for inflation, recession, and the near certainty of a higher cost of capital. We have experienced excess capital at low cost. That has turned upside down. The cost of capital will increase, and demand will be high. It is needed to finance the deficit, for infrastructure, and for things like helping Ukraine, fending off climate change, and reshoring supply chains—all of which are capital intensive.

LOOKING FORWARD TO BAD TIMES

It's not only pessimists who expect bad times ahead. Dave Flitman, CEO of Builders FirstSource, a Dallas-based distributor of building materials and maker of manufactured components, runs a thriving business that he believes has a huge runway. Yet his positive vision for the company is based on a range of dour predictions about the economy, ranging from bad to much worse.

Builders FirstSource completed a merger with BMC Stock Holdings, another big player in the building-materials market, in January 2021, creating the largest building-materials distributor in the United States and a Fortune 200 behemoth. While leading through the COVID-19 pandemic and merger integration, the company was hit with tremendous supply chain challenges. Demand for housing rose as people began to realize they could work from home and needed more space.

"Housing demand and starts in 2021 spiked to the highest level in 14 years," Flitman says. "The supply chain just was not ready for it. Lead times for every material from lumber and hardware to doors and windows stretched from three or four weeks to 20 to 24 weeks. Imagine a large homebuilder having to tell us six months in advance how many windows and doors they were going to need! It created chaos. And, of course, costs were rising sharply as a result of the spike in demand and the constrained supply chain."

The company navigated through it all very well, but Flitman and his team kept their eye on the drivers of demand in their industry: mainly new housing starts, which are strongly linked to mortgage rates. From January to July 2022, mortgage rates nearly doubled and went from less than 3% to 5.7%. Who was driving a lot of the housing growth? Millennials. They were buying their first home or a step-up home with room for kids and some green space and comparing the cost of a mortgage to rent.

"So we were watching those changes closely. We knew that the average cost of a house had gone from $260,000 in 2018 to $410,000 in May 2022," Flitman explains. "Then you layer on top of that the fact that mortgage rates had doubled over six months. We started to see early that the industry was going to start to slow down, and we started to plan for the bad times during the good times." Builders FirstSource delivered a record $1.5 billion in adjusted EBITDA on $6.9 billion in sales in the second quarter of 2022 and repurchased 25% of its outstanding shares over the prior 12 months.

The team mapped out targets and specific actions they would take depending on the depth of the downturn in housing—a 10%, 25%, or 40% reduction—and shared their plan with the board. Those items included a $100 million productivity target, which would be achieved by reducing organizational layers, optimizing driver turnaround time in the yards, and a host of other activities. They also planned to re-engineer business practices to gain efficiency.

They restructured their debt to push maturities out to 2032 and identified the projects they would curtail in a slower market environment. They froze headcount but planned what portion of variable costs they would need to cut depending on the degree of the downturn. They were determined to stay focused on customers but would prioritize them based on which ones would remain profitable in leaner times. "We're not bulletproof," Flitman told us. "And I wanted our team to think through all potential outcomes so we're ready for whatever comes our way."

Flitman accelerated communications of all types (email, videos, town halls) to keep his nearly 30,000 team members with him along the journey. "I've started to change the tone a little about what we think the future will hold," he says. "People saw that inflation hit 9.1% in June 2022, so they know what is coming, and they need to know we're on it.

"I don't wish for bad things, and I don't want a recession. But we're positioning our company to get through that time period. Our team can outperform in any market, and that is my goal."

CHAPTER 3

Pay Attention To Cash

Cash management is the number-one risk to your business and the key to managing it safely through inflationary times. You need to have a clear picture at all times of where cash is coming from and where it is going to, with a view of how those flows will change in the coming quarters. You should be seeking ways to reduce costs and lower the break-even point, but the important shift is to focus on the balance sheet, not just the P&L. Orient yourself to think in terms of cash profits, not paper profits or percentages.

If you're not watching cash and taking steps to ensure you have enough of it, you are putting your business on shaky ground. As inflation persists, many items you consider done deals could come to haunt you. For example, if you have contracts to sell at fixed prices with no such assurances on the cost side, you are headed for trouble. If you have variable-rate loans or need to borrow money going forward but don't have a plan to cover higher cash payments, you could likewise be in trouble. If you are in an industry that relies heavily on energy, directly or indirectly, you could also be in trouble.

And don't forget that customers consume cash in the form of receivables, inventory, and production, some more than others. A customer that pays receivables in 275 days might not be worth having, even if you get a hefty margin. A large U.S. bank chose to drop some big commercial customers when it realized the disproportionate impact they had on the bank's balance sheet. Things look very different when you analyze profitability on the basis of a margin measured in percentage points versus profitability measured on the basis of net cash.

You have to know how cash is flowing and learn where it typically gets trapped, especially as rising interest rates slow economic growth. You will want to scrutinize how you use cash to build the business and keep it running, whether as operating expenses (Opex) or capital expenditures (Capex). All of your business planning and forecasts should include an analysis of cash, and you should revisit the investments you already planned with an eye toward cash.

CASH USAGE

Never have early warning signals and preemptive action been more useful to a company than in protecting cash as inflation clouds gathered. In the U.S., people were waking up to inflation warnings around February 2022, but DK Agarwal says Indorama Ventures picked up on it in late 2020 and started taking action in 2021. "We thought the stimulus packages and other factors would put unnecessary pressure on interest rates," he told us. "We always try to have proper risk management, so when we saw concrete early warning signals that there was too much money in the system, we knew inflation was going to come and that we had to fix the interest rate on our debt."

In 2021, Indorama Ventures locked in about 68% of its debt on a fixed basis, with some maturities as long as seven years. "So our risk is only the 32% that is floating," Agarwal explains. The company also locked in some lines of credit. "We created $300 to $400 million more liquidity, so today we have about $2 billion. Liquidity is very important to us, because you never know when oil will go to $200 a barrel."

Energy was not the only input Indorama Ventures was concerned about. Agarwal noticed other issues brewing as he traveled the world in the course of his work. He saw an acute shortage of people in the world, among white-collar workers but even more so among blue-collar workers. When he traveled to Brazil and visited with banks there, he learned that interest rates had gone from 2% to 10.5% in just one year. Fearful of the hyperinflation Brazil had experienced in past decades, policymakers were taking an aggressive stance to contain it.

Even if you missed the earliest signs of inflation, the sooner you fix the balance sheet to protect cash, the better. In a period of rising inflation, debt is a killer. You might think it's fine to keep the debt you have because it is low-priced. But you have to consider whether you can actually service that debt. Will inflation shrink your cash margins? If you can't generate as much cash as you did before, then even low-priced debt will be a problem.

Among the things that have not changed from earlier bouts with inflation is the risk of insolvency. Bankruptcies rose steadily in the early 1980s before the Federal Reserve got inflation under control. It can happen again to the unwary. Watch your balance sheet and safeguard your liquidity.

BEWARE OF CASH TRAPS IN WORKING CAPITAL

The most insidious aspect of inflation is how it affects working capital. The cost of money has been so low and steady for so long that you probably never had to think much about the relationship between revenue growth and working capital. Now you do.

Any attempt to grow your business or even sustain it at the current level will consume cash in accounts receivable and inventory, two major components of working capital. That additional cash has to come from somewhere. In high inflation, the options narrow. It is harder to generate cash profits, and at the same time it costs more to borrow money.

A disciplined approach to cash and working capital is always good business practice, but for a whole generation of leaders, the consequences of ignoring it have been nil. Having managed multiple companies through crisis situations, DuPont CEO Ed Breen was laser focused on cash. Together with his CFO Lori Koch, who had extensive experience in operational finance, and Raj Ratnakar, who had many years of experience at Danaher, a company known for its operational discipline, Breen kicked off an aggressive plan to reduce cash consumption across the company.

"We are obsessed about cash. We watch it on a weekly and even daily basis," Ratnakar says. "That focus started before COVID, and it has really helped us as inflation picked up. We've been continually improving working capital and have reduced capital expenditure consumption."

That improvement in working capital includes making sure that accounts receivable don't get stretched. Customers almost always want to extend the terms of their payments. In inflation, some will test the limits—pushing from 60 days to 90 and even to 180 or more. Unless you are vigilant about what is happening to those accounts and manage those customer relationships, your accounts receivable will become a cash trap. Now imagine that as inflation persists, some customers get into serious financial trouble. Some may even default. How does that affect your cash situation?

"When the cost of capital is near zero, it doesn't cost you a lot to give a customer a little better terms to get more business," Ratnakar says. "Our general managers generally think, 'If it takes an extra 30 days, it's really not going to kill us. Those extra days don't cost us much, and we might as well get a point of market share, so great!' "

The equation has now shifted. You have to know the real cost and risk of allowing companies to extend their payments. Business-to-business companies should start looking right now at which customers have high debt or hugely inflated costs that could make them short of cash. They're the ones that could hurt you. Reach out to them immediately, and work with them on payment plans. TVS Motors, which manufactures two- and three-wheeled motor bikes in India, used to offer dealers financing. Now, it accepts only cash in hand and helps dealers find financing elsewhere.

To help leaders across the organization manage accounts receivable, DuPont standardized a set of metrics for it. For example, the company tracked the percentage of receivables that were past due. "When you tell a business leader they have to improve accounts receivable, they're not sure how to go about it," Ratnakar says. "So we translated broad targets for accounts receivable balances and for DSO [Days Sales Outstanding] into tangible operational improvements we could measure—for example, the past-due percentage by customer segments. We educated leaders on 'what good looks like' using industry benchmarks to show how much room remained for improvement. And finally, we gave them a concrete toolkit of best practices to help them execute the program."

DuPont is, of course, a huge business, and payment terms vary among the businesses. But standardized metrics have several benefits, including visibility and comparability. Ratnakar notes, "When you show that one business had 1.5% past dues and improved it to .9%, while another had 15% past dues and got it to 12%, it can be motivating."

He continues, "When we see that some salespeople are doing a better job than other salespeople, or one branch manager or regional manager is able to do better, we can start asking, 'Why is that?' If payments are always late in one segment, you might hear something like, 'Oh, payments are always late in Asia.' Then we can go and tell them that in a different product segment, Asia is actually the best performer.

"A combination of metrics and tools helps the sales force see the points of leverage. If you have lower-margin customers with greater terms, there's something wrong with that. Or if you're giving the less profitable customer two times the payment terms when another customer delivers three times as much profits and pays on time, what's the justification? You can start to see where the bad customers are, and with inflation, that's highly relevant."

Along with accounts receivable, inventory was on DuPont's radar screen as it set targets for improving working capital. "The problem with inventory during inflation is two-fold," Ratnakar explains. "As with accounts receivables, it consumes precious cash that is more expensive, and if you have large inventory positions when raw material prices are increasing, you risk hits to profitability when prices revert back. Damage comes if you end up having to sell end products at low prices from inventory that was built up in a high-cost environment."

Inventory becomes a cash trap quickly in inflation. Yet, in an environment of scarcity and/or rising costs, companies are tempted to stock up for fear that things will be unavailable or more expensive going forward. Recession will only exacerbate the problem. In late spring 2022, both Walmart and Target were stuck with high inventories of general merchandise when inflation forced consumers to spend more on food, and it was clear that those inventories would need to be sold at a discount.

The important point is that you must use whatever means you can to keep inventory low while still meeting customers' needs, and you must recognize that as revenues grow, inventory will grow and consume cash. Digital technology will be enormously helpful, but other actions, such as narrowing the range of products or increasing velocity, are also useful. A real-estate business pushed to finish projects faster and sell them sooner, even at a lower price, because inflation creates higher holding costs.

Decisions about what inventory levels are appropriate and how to manage any increased use of cash should be mediated among finance, manufacturing, purchasing, sales and marketing. It's easy to see why those who use algorithms to help manage inventories will have an edge.

REPRIORITIZE AND PLAN
YOUR USE OF CASH

So, you've developed a strategy, made some investments, and planned others. Have you reconsidered the cash they will generate or consume under inflation?

However well reasoned your original plan, you should go through it now on a cash basis and look at the *cumulative* effect of inflation. You have no choice but to think long term. Unless we have a recession, there is no step change in inflation. Let's say inflation is 7% this year, and the Fed increases interest rates by 2% and does some quantitative tightening, so inflation slows to 5%. Then say it goes to 4%. That will take you to a 17% increase cumulatively over just those few years. Are you sure you will have the cash to fund the current slate of initiatives?

Almost 50 years ago, Ram was asked to design and teach a course on "coping with inflation"—nicknamed COIN—at General Electric's famous learning center in Crotonville, New

York. The issue was cash. Inflation had seemed to come out of nowhere and, as now, many terrific general managers lacked experience dealing with it. Reginald Jones, CEO at the time, saw that the company was running out of cash and jeopardizing GE's cherished AAA credit rating. He commissioned Ram to teach some 900 GE executives, roughly 30 at a time, how to deal with inflation and get a grip on cash.

Ram's teaching always has a practical bent, so he asked the participants to make a cash flow projection going forward under different inflationary rates. Those scenarios had to include one based on a very conservative forecast for cash generation combined with inflated cash outflows in the next four quarters. People took action, some of them slowing down or scaling back their plans, to stay cash positive even under a worst-case scenario, and GE preserved its blue-chip status.

Planning must include cash adjusted for inflation and must also be more granular and future oriented. Quarterly planning is not enough. The time horizon should be two or three years so inflation's cumulative effects are baked in. Detailed cost analysis must be institutionalized, forward looking, and shared across the organization, particularly with sales and marketing executives who need that information for pricing.

There are always too many demands on cash. You have to keep the business going, so think through what is required to sustain it and win against competition. Advertising money?

Short-term innovation to justify higher margin products? Expenditures for reducing costs and break-even points?

You may have to spend on digitalization so you can do dynamic pricing, better match supply and demand, or segment customers. You have to be concerned about cybersecurity. Maybe you need to build capacity or relocate your supply chain. You have to maintain the plant and equipment, something you'll be tempted to postpone—but shouldn't. Then there are longer-term demands, such as ESG. After all, sustainability is not going away, and it requires a lot of investment.

All of these things are competing for cash, whether in the form of operating expenses (Opex) or capital expenditures (Capex). You can set an ambitious goal to improve working capital, as DuPont did, but you will still have to make hard choices.

A simple framework, as below, can help you prioritize how cash should be allocated:

1. Continuity of the business

2. Digitalization of the business

3. Fixing bottlenecks and removing frictions in the supply chain

4. Focused innovation

5. Capex for building essential capacity

CHAPTER 4

Change Your Pricing Approach—Fast

Pricing may have been a relatively low priority over the past decade, but under inflation it is central to survival. Whether you're expecting more inflation, recession, stagflation, or a return to growth, you should fully understand how pricing affects your moneymaking and relationships with customers. It's not just that you have to raise prices, which you almost certainly do; you may have to revise your whole approach to pricing.

This economic era demands a break from past practices, even those that have worked fine so far. Maybe your sales are largely transactional, but now a subscription-based approach works better. Maybe you've ruled out surcharges, but now they make sense. Revisit your choices.

The range of options on pricing is likely wider than you think, and the options you choose matter more than you think.

Take the example of two lumber distribution businesses, both owned by the same private equity firm. You might recall reading about the skyrocketing cost of lumber and wild fluctuations in supply in 2021 at the same time home construction was picking up. Both lumber distribution companies in the PE's portfolio had to contend with those inflated prices, but one of the businesses fared much better than the other because of its thoughtful approach to pricing.

Distributor A had an approach that set prices based on an index with a fixed margin percentage automatically added in. When the cost of lumber took off, the distributor's prices got adjusted right away with no lag time. Because the percentage markup remained fixed, higher costs led to higher prices, which led to more cash coming in. As Adam Echter, partner at pricing consultancy Simon-Kucher & Partners, explains, "Because 40% of $100 is $40 but 40% of $200 is $80 and so on, the more costs went up, the more cash came in. Money was just falling from the sky, and EBITDA blew up beyond the PE company's wildest imagination."[1]

Distributor B's story was different. It had a solid business, but its reliance on negotiations with individual customers to

1 Adam Echter provided this and several other case examples in this chapter and generously shared with us the deep expertise of Simon-Kucher & Partners, a renowned global consultancy that specializes in pricing. That learning is reflected throughout this chapter. See also www.simon-kucher. com for more in-depth material on pricing.

set prices made it hard to keep up with continually rising costs. Distributor A came through that volatile period with resources to acquire weaker players. Distributor B was weakened.

Regardless of where you sit today, inflation gives you the opportunity to evolve the pricing function and build a new capability for your company. Accelerate your pace of price changes, but be thoughtful about how you implement them so you don't wear down your sales force or alienate customers.

EXPAND YOUR RANGE OF OPTIONS

Inflation is an opportunity to improve your approach to pricing. We use the word *approach* broadly, to include the following:

1. **Your pricing mode**—Are sales transactional, subscription based, or contractual?

2. **Your pricing method**—Do you use dynamic pricing, peer pricing, index pricing, or custom negotiations?

3. **Your pricing model**—Are prices derived by a desire to fill a factory, maintain a target margin, hit a list price, or extract an estimated value?

4. **Your pricing strategy**—Do you set prices with the intent to penetrate a market, retain a customer base, or maximize value extraction?

However you combined these elements in the past, you should consider whether a shift might work better in current times. Making a switch was a way out of trouble for a crane manufacturer in the wake of the 2008–2009 financial crisis. When the economy slumped, shipping took a big hit, and so did the demand for the cranes that move containers on and off ships. The company had already sunk a lot of money into building the cranes, which cost millions of dollars, and couldn't shut down production without risking huge losses and startup costs—yet orders were getting cancelled one after the other.

Their solution was to place the cranes at the ports and charge a price for every container that was moved. Shipping companies saved money because they paid only for what they used and didn't have to invest a lot of money up front. The crane manufacturer had some income, and when shipping volume returned four or five years later, it had a very profitable business anchored to a high price-per-container-moves metric that had been established when volumes were low. Instead of seeing the cranes inflate away in value and taking a huge sunk cost, the company changed its pricing approach and was ready when the economy rebounded.

Some approaches will fare better than others in inflation:

- If your company is transactional (like a street vendor exchanging an apple for a dollar), has a cost-plus pricing strategy (adding in 40% of the cost to arrive at a price), and uses an index (for example, for the cost of a key raw material), it is well positioned for inflation. It will pass inflation straight through.

- If your mission is to maintain a 10% margin, the company has real-time information on inputs like plastics and energy, and you have contracts that allow you to reprice on that basis, you too are relatively sheltered from inflating costs.

- Software or pharmaceutical companies have low incremental costs and tend to use value-based pricing with high margins. Unless they are locked into long-term contracts, they likely have enough cushion in their margin to absorb cost fluctuations.

- A maker of, say, brass plumbing fittings that uses cost-plus pricing and then negotiates a lot of discounts might be wise to use an index for the inflationary effects of copper or brass. Or, if it is transaction based, it could use a bidding or auction approach to boost prices and recoup costs when demand is greater than supply.

Other combinations are dangerous in inflation. Take, for example, a contract business where you signed a five-year contract two years ago, pre-inflation, aimed at keeping your factory at full capacity. You rely on customer negotiations and have no systems to reprice. Unless you change something, you're at high risk of burning through cash and going bankrupt.

Although there is no one approach that suits every business, more companies should consider a shift to value-based pricing. Echter notes that the difficult task of having to renegotiate a contract is a great opportunity to move to a value-based approach: "When you have to break a truly untenable contract, you find out how valuable you are to the other party."

If you plan to go with cost-plus, be sure your costs are properly measured. Remember, no gross margin, no lunch. You must make a profit to stay in business, so think of that profit as a necessary cost you have to cover. Echter recalls a lesson shared from Simon-Kucher & Partners' founder and namesake, Hermann Simon: "When a stubborn client insists on a cost-plus price, just look at your profit margin as the cost of staying in business."

GRASP THE URGENCY OF PRICE INCREASES

Unless you pick up the pace of price changes, you could seriously miss cash and earnings that you can never recover. Across an industry, someone will be first to make a move. If you leave it to sales and marketing alone, you may never get the price increases you need, let alone be first in line. They may stall because they don't want to lose the customer or dread getting serious pushback from them.

The dominant psychology of sales and marketing for the past decade has been to capture as many customers as possible and make every sale one can, without thinking too hard about whether the sale is profitable or the customer is sound. There's been a psychological aversion to raising prices.

Senior leaders have to address this issue head on. It's one thing to know that price increases are in order and another to see that those changes are made promptly. As Raj Ratnakar at DuPont says, "When we tell salespeople that we need to raise prices by 10% or 15%—and in some of our products, by 30%—the salesperson has to walk into a customer and explain that what would be a 1% to 2% increase in a normal year will now be 30% this year. It is not easy for the culture in the industrial world to take in.

"As a whole, we've done a good job on this front. And some of the businesses have been outstanding in how they've delivered quickly, but some have lagged, and one is really struggling. It's just culturally not in them."

When DuPont chose to be among the first in its industries to raise prices, common concerns about losing market share didn't pan out. Ratnakar explains, "We have a long tradition of having the trust and respect of customers, and we wanted to maintain that. Everything starts with open and honest communications with customers. We want customers to know it is happening for very specific reasons and that the pricing policies are therefore fair. We also want them to know that such movements are across the board, that they are not being uniquely targeted.

"Over the past year, in some product categories we have had to implement multiple price increases. Every time, we clearly laid out the rationale to our customers. While none of them like price increases, they do trust us and know that every player is facing the same set of problems. Shifting business to another player just for a slightly lower price and losing out on all the reasons they picked DuPont in the first place—like quality and supply reliability—is short sighted; competitors may be slow to react, but it is a matter of time before they follow with price increases of their own. On the other hand, using a crisis to increase prices unfairly can be detrimental to long-term growth, so DuPont never participates in such irrational moves that risk losing trust."

During supply disruptions and inflation, it is common for market leaders in some industries to communicate to the market that price increases are coming. Different companies use different approaches, such as published rate books, press releases, or open letters to customers. That helps customers prepare and also gives competitors that are facing the same problems some relief. They allow themselves to follow suit, heading off a war for market share in the middle of a difficult macro situation.

BIG PRICE JUMPS VERSUS FREQUENT SMALLER ONES

Maybe you already faced reality and made a big boost to your prices. In a changing economic environment, you cannot consider any price change to be one and done. Changing prices now has to be routine, timely, and linked as tightly as possible to current realities.

Developing a cadence of more frequent price changes will pay off better than playing catchup with one big price increase sometime later. Big jumps will make you lose a chunk of customers, more than if you had raised prices in smaller increments right along. Businesses that try to wait out inflation or that make a big change just once will find themselves needing to make an unpleasant and customer-losing big price adjustment down the line.

Don't throw up your hands just because you have contracts that fix prices for a period of time and have no explicit accommodation to reset them, even as rising commodity costs and scarcities make those contracts money losers. Echter says that Simon-Kucher & Partners has been getting a lot of calls asking for help in breaking contracts. He has seen that when senior executives reach out to customers and have honest discussions about their dilemma, lo and behold, customers have accepted the new reality and allowed for renegotiation.

They will likely pass those increases onto their customers, which are next in the value chain.

Any contracts you renegotiate now should have more frequent repricing built in. "Nothing precludes going to customers out of cycle and negotiating with them," says Karen Flynn, head of Commercial Operations at Catalent. "We did that, saying that, 'yes, we have annual mechanisms, but these are extraordinary times.' We went to the table with a rationale for getting other increases in place outside of those dictated by the terms of the contract. In times of business pressures, we have to do what we can to offset the cost increases, so we knew we had to have those discussions with customers."

Indorama Ventures was equally successful with updating contracts. CEO and CFO DK Agarwal says they worked with major customers to change the terms when contracts were coming up for renewal. "We now have inflation factored in, so if it rises, we build it into the price. We use the CPI and a fuel index or the price of gas in some contracts so it links to energy and raw materials. That way our margins are protected."

Accelerating the cadence of price changes allows you to also adjust for event-driven challenges, whether it's a major supplier going offline due to COVID lockdowns, a supply chain glitch from a ship getting stuck in a canal, or a factory being flooded in a tsunami—all of which have actually happened. When unusually cold temperatures in Texas took much of the U.S. plastics industry offline in February 2021, the price response was immediate. Trying to claw back margin in a negotiation ten months later would have been hard for customers to accept; by then they would have been convinced that you could absorb the margin compression.

REVISIT THE PRICING TACTICS IN YOUR TOOLKIT

A review of your pricing approach goes beyond the price itself to include surcharges, fees, and terms and conditions. Some companies have avoided surcharges, partly because they can be seen as temporary. But they are a useful tool for recovering costs that have newly erupted and getting cash sooner. It might take three or four months to approve a new price sheet, but a CFO can implement a surcharge overnight in many cases, and it spares the sales force from yet another discussion about price.

Consider how the transport of Ukraine's wheat is being affected by Russia's blockade of ports in the Black Sea. Countries are working to build capacity to transport it to Europe by road or rail. We should expect to see a surcharge for transportation, along with inflated prices for wheat due to the supply constraints.

Surcharges can also apply to specific things you are already doing, such as hazardous-waste disposal or nonstandard delivery. When you link the surcharge to an activity, it tends to land well with customers and translates into an immediate profit. A HVAC repair facility that was already disposing of refrigerant in an ecological way was able to boost profits by adding a surcharge for doing so.

Anytime a customer asks for something out of the ordinary, it is an opportunity to add a surcharge or fee. A red container versus a blue one, a valve on the left versus the right—such requests are an indication of what the customer values and is probably willing to pay for.

Contract terms are another avenue for adding revenue and cash that is urgently needed in inflation. Many existing contracts have unenforced terms originally put in to avoid costs, such as minimum order quantities or partial truck loads. Enforcing them is something you can do quickly. For new or renewing contracts, shortening the payment terms or asking customers to prepay in exchange for guaranteed allocations during supply constraints will be a big boon to your cash management.

Both what to charge for and how much to charge should be up for discussion. Get the team to make a list of possible surcharges, then narrow it down to five or six items. When it comes to deciding how much to charge, look at it through the value lens: What is it worth to the customer? In establishing a surcharge for hazardous-waste disposal, a company estimated it should charge about $8. Then they had Simon-Kucher &

Partners speak to the markets, which showed that the value customers placed on it was greater than $50.

A test will verify whether your proposed number will actually be acceptable. The company that installed the hazardous-waste surcharge had 85% adherence on all surcharges six months later.

CUSTOMER SEGMENTATION

You will get the most benefit by tailoring your pricing approach to customer segments. Data gathered digitally can help you decide which customers to focus on and what pricing approach to use, but segmentation will improve if you combine data with human judgment from top management and the sales force working together.

A new CEO joined an outdoor products company in 2018. As she examined the business, she realized that all their customers were getting the same white-glove service and being charged in the same way, although those relationships were vastly different. She set out to create a new pricing mechanism and only apply it to some customer segments.

The company designed a mechanism that would react as soon as a supplier indicated that a price change was coming, whether it was for products made of wood, hard-coil steel, or PVC, and immediately adjust prices. Then it separated its customers into segments, using the 80/20 rule to define the bulk of customers that were most important to it. The company decided to apply the new pricing mechanism to its biggest, most valued customers. This segment would continue to get white-glove service, and prices would be quickly updated and value based. For smaller accounts, the ones that made purchases because the price was low or products weren't available elsewhere, the company would provide only limited service and swiftly raise prices based on leading index trends until the product was sold out.

The new pricing approach took time to develop, which the CEO used to bring the sales force and others at the company on board. By 2020, it was ready to launch, and the timing was auspicious. Wood, metal, and PVC—all of which were components the company used—were struck by inflation to some degree, so costs jumped.

The pricing mechanism, however, protected the company from inflation's devastating effects. It was, in fact, *preemptive.* That is, the price of existing inventory was based not on its cost at the time it was purchased but rather on what the cost would be to replace it now. If the inventory cost $100 at the time but now costs $150, the price would jump to $150 plus a markup.

A clear understanding of what customers valued is part of what made this pricing approach successful. The company had a stellar reputation for reliability, which was precious in a time of scarcity. Although competitors drew customers with lower prices, they often cancelled orders, leaving the customer high and dry. To a segment of customers, reliable delivery and availability were more important than the price point.

Segmentation takes time and can be tedious, but it paves the way for personalization. Although digital tools always help, segmentation is often done without fancy software. When Ram first visited IBM in the 1970s, he wondered why the pricing department was so large. He learned from a former student who worked there that the pricing experts worked closely with the salespeople to personalize each account. The outdoor products company CEO did the same; she set up weekly meetings and rolled through every single account to keep up on which customers were on top and how to treat them differently. Personalization gives you a chance to bundle products, redesign offerings, or provide different levels of service.

Before inflation reared up in a big way, the owner of the outdoor products company set an EBITDA target for it and a second, unrelated business. The outdoor products company's success came sooner than expected and completely overshadowed the second business. It almost doubled EBITDA, achieving in one year what the owner had hoped to achieve in five years.

BEWARE OF SALES FORCE FATIGUE

Let's assume you're ahead of the curve and have been repricing quickly and frequently. Your sales force will be delivering most of those increases to the customer. So now you have to face a different inflation-driven challenge: sales force fatigue. Running a legacy repricing process faster and faster will exhaust your team.

Automating price adjustments, perhaps for a select segment of customers, will relieve the pressure. As one manager put it, "People who do a small amount of business with us can be just as mean as big accounts." A solution at his company was to use dynamic pricing for small accounts and free up salespeople to negotiate with the bigger ones.

There is such a thing as price fatigue as well. This inflationary period is just getting started, and already we've seen cost increases work their way through the value chain. As every player in the chain tries to preserve his or her nominal dollars or percentage profit, higher prices work their way from one link in the chain to the next, moving relentlessly toward the consumer and end user. At some point, the end user can't absorb it and seeks an alternative or does without. This won't happen in every category, but it will surely happen in some.

Regardless of where you are in the chain, when price increases hit a dead end they become your problem. You should have three lines of pursuit: search for ways to reduce costs not just within your four walls but across the value chain, create new kinds of value, and help customers do the same. Chapters five and six will give you ideas how.

CHAPTER 5

Find Cost Cuts That Build The Business

When Catalent was battling for highly specialized talent in a tight marketplace, the company had no choice but to raise compensation. Facing that reality, CEO John Chiminski launched a company-wide search for cost reductions in other parts of the business, dubbed Total Cost Excellence. He created multiple teams to explore a full range of options. One team, led by the head of HR, focused on professional services; another, led by a quality leader and a scientist together, looked at spending in the labs; a third looked at manufacturing materials; a fourth looked at maintenance for production equipment and replacement parts; another focused on IT; and yet another dug into travel and expenses.

As you cope with inflation you'll run up against some costs that are impossible to control, whether it's because the material is rare, the trading floor sets the price of a commodity, or front-line workers have a multitude of options. Do what Catalent did: go beyond the obvious targets and consider all the direct and indirect costs strung across the company. How could they be reduced?

Then go further. Those incremental savings will add up and help you weather rising costs, but you should also step back and ask a different question: Do I have to make a more radical change to reduce my costs and/or cash consumption?

A step/jump in reducing costs might come from looking beyond the boundaries of your business and working with others in the value chain. When one link in the chain is affected, others are too. Or you might have to completely revise your geographic footprint, for people as well as sourcing.

The point is to get through an inflationary period with customers intact and with a stronger business than before. That comes from keeping customers top of mind and searching for things you can do to help them get through. At the same time, you should work with the other side of the value chain to help suppliers cut whatever costs they can control.

If you think bigger and more broadly and don't back away from a bold change, you'll see how inflation creates a chance for your company to leap ahead.

CUTTING COSTS, ADDING VALUE

Apparel, footwear, and other consumer staples are among the industries that have been severely challenged by both the pandemic and inflation. Many players in the supply chains for those industries are based in Southeast Asian countries such as Sri Lanka, Vietnam, Bangladesh, and India. As consumer demand dropped precipitously, cash froze up, and exports dwindled. Companies and their domestic economies were badly hurt. When Ram interviewed leaders at several of these companies in mid-2022, most were struggling. One company, a medium-sized player in the middle of the footwear supply chain, was the exception. The CEO of the shoe company told Ram, "We see the positive side of inflation. We are using it to demonstrate our differentiation."

The CEO knew that its customers—the companies next in the value chain—were still recovering, so raising prices to pass along cost increases was not a realistic option. He asked his team to take out costs wherever they could, with one caveat: he would not support cuts that weakened the business, either their own or those of their customers or the subcontractors that manufactured their products. That declaration took many typical cost cuts off the table and spurred more creative thinking.

The search for savings led the CEO and his team to make some internal changes that, yes, saved some money, but also made the company operate more efficiently. One such change was reducing organizational layers from nine to six. The CEO began the reorganization by cutting two layers at the top. Once the company had digested that change, he eliminated a middle layer as well. The lower layers were preserved because the CEO did not want to disrupt any of the people who interface with customers directly and had built trustworthy relationships with them.

Those internal changes translated into faster decisions and approvals, and the company became more responsive to customers' requests, a change customers appreciated—and said so. But it was just a start.

BOTH SIDES OF THE VALUE CHAIN

In his determination to thrive despite the difficult circumstances, the CEO pressed the team to expand their vision beyond the company's own four walls. "I saw an opportunity for us by taking a broader view. I wanted us to think about suppliers and customers as well as our own company," he said. "Competitors are 100% focused on reducing cost and generating cash internally just to survive. But if we strengthen the whole end-to-end value chain, we can win the game for the future."

The team latched onto the concept of making both sides of the value chain—their customers and their suppliers—stronger so the entire chain would prosper. When they saw the factors of production rising, things like gasoline and fuel oil used to convert raw materials into components, they knew everything would soon be more expensive. They wanted their customers to be prepared, so they urged them to focus on seasonal purchases and make commitments early to get ahead of the cost increases. Taking a more disciplined approach to forecasting, they contended, would reduce inventory and conserve cash across the supply chain and help prevent cost increases and supply disruptions.

The management team also tried to help its contractors with their manufacturing processes. About 50% of the cost of shoe manufacturing is for C&M, the vernacular for cutting and making the basic product. Inefficient use of production capacity drives C&M costs higher. On the flip side, optimizing capacity reduces costs. The team knew that if they could help improve operations at the factories, customers would be better able to handle the cost increases that were externally driven. Accounts receivable would ease, and again, the whole chain would be on firmer ground.

Then the team took a similar stance with their suppliers. The CEO explains, "We looked at how our suppliers optimized their capacity, and we saw that if we could help them stretch their assets, it would reduce more cost. By helping them manage their capacity, pricing would be more favorable for us. Our customers, and our customers' customers, would stand to benefit."

NEW SOURCING FRONTIERS

The quest to lower costs and improve the business also led the shoe company to question its geographic footprint. The team didn't just assume that the contract manufacturers the company used in China or India or Indonesia had the lowest costs. They felt compelled to explore other countries and continents.

They saw Mexico and some Caribbean countries as a new possibility. Production there would allow faster delivery of products to customers in the U.S., the biggest product market. Shorter lead times meant fewer markdowns of footwear that might have missed a season or a trend, therefore improving moneymaking.

NEW WAYS OF WORKING

As the CEO reconsidered where to locate sourcing and production, he also reconsidered the location of people. That line of thought led to a major shift in some key jobs.

Until then, managers who oversaw large customer accounts had been based in major cities across Asia, where the cost of living was relatively high. They were distant from the company's production facilities, which were generally in lower-cost locations. The CEO made the decision to move some people from the high-cost places to the lower-cost places, where products were actually produced, and carved out a new, broader set of responsibilities.

Moving people to lower-cost areas reduced costs and solved a vexing problem.

The sales-manager job had evolved to be essentially that of an order-taker. Managers would work out an agreement with a customer and dump it on the production facilities where it would be executed. Those at the receiving end would think, "I can't fill this order with this kind of cost structure," or, "This lead time is not realistic." The lack of consultation created a lot of friction.

"So we decided to make the production facilities in each country a separate profit and loss center, with a person in charge of filling all the orders for that country," the CEO explained. "We moved people from the high-cost cities to the new locations and put them in a central role. He or she fields all the orders and fits them in, weighing how best to optimize the allocation of resources against various customers' needs."

The benefit of having people on the ground who understand customer demands as well as production constraints was soon evident. "If you're in a city talking with customers, you're not in tune with production," the CEO says. "But if you're in Vietnam and a problem pops up, you can nip it in the bud. You can transfer orders, make changes, and make decisions based on real-time, unfiltered information with a deep understanding of how to meet customer needs."

What's clear from all that this company has going on is that in a high-inflation environment, you've got to help your customers deal with rising costs, even as you fight to contain them. You also have to work with suppliers because cost incurred on that side of the value chain will affect players at every step that follows. Along the way, you should search for ways to add value, not just cut costs, on both sides of the value chain. It's all connected.

CHAPTER 6

Renew Your Business Model

The cumulative effects of inflation are leading to a world of lower consumption overall, one in which some consumer behavior will have changed permanently. There will not be a return to what we've known. Some segments—even some industries—will have shrunk, and some new ones may have appeared. As you adjust your pricing, product offerings, costs, and cash flow along the way, at some point your business model might reach a breaking point.

To thrive in the emerging world of lower consumption and slower growth, you will almost certainly need a new business model. You should focus on it now.

Don't wait for mountains of evidence that the current business model isn't working. Be honest: Is your most lucrative market evaporating? Are the new market segments you've targeted still there, and at the same price points? You may be convinced that demand for your services will return to what it was, but when? Can you really wait it out? Will something more appealing have sprung up in the meantime? Pool your observations, look at data and trends, and start to think about how you will reinvent the business model.

Creating a new business model may be as new to you as inflation. Many CEOs have had long tenures without having to change it. But don't ignore the necessity.

Remember that even if you are slow to recognize that the business model is breaking, investors won't be. Declining or persistently stagnant earnings with no sign of future building will begin to affect your market valuation. With that comes another insidious impact: you'll have to use more cash for things like pension funding. When resources start to dwindle, you have fewer options to make a change.

THE ESSENCE OF A BUSINESS MODEL

When you change the elements of your business model—your sources of revenue, customer mix, product mix, geographic footprint, cost structure, and moneymaking model—the whole thing can begin to unravel, and moneymaking breaks down. That's when you've got real troubles.

The mental challenge is to conceptualize how the key elements could work together differently. If you put moneymaking first and foremost, you'll short-change customers and your future. When inflation raged in the 1970s, some beverage and food companies kept prices the same but cut the size of their soda cans or candy bars, as if customers wouldn't notice. Customers did notice. They felt cheated, and the brands were damaged for years.

At the same time, if you give customers the same thing at the same price despite rising costs, your moneymaking will erode. If you're a publicly traded company, you'll lose investors and lack investment capital, and quality will begin to decline. You'll be on a downward slide.

To win in profitable customer segments, you need innovation. How will you fund it? Digitalization will help you reduce waste and therefore cost. It will help you customize products and services and therefore boost revenue and cash. It also makes innovation cheaper and more efficient. Again, how will you fund it?

Keep iterating your conception of the business model until your products, customers, and business portfolios work with your moneymaking formula—your need for positive cash flow, gross margin, and profitable growth that can fund critical investments.

CHANGING THE MIX

No business model lasts forever. As consumer behavior changes and competitors change their products and services, your markets get redefined by default, even if you do nothing. Be ready by rethinking all the places and ways you currently play.

Customer segments. The need for cash might force you to drop customers that cannot keep up with payments to you, and price increases might drive some customers away. Are there new segments emerging where you don't compete yet? Are there some you need to redefine to better understand their needs?

Product mix. Look at your current mix with fresh eyes. In an era of free-spending consumers, versions of products and services tend to proliferate. The sheer number of SKUs (stock keeping units) can create all kinds of complexity that works against efficient management of production and cash. It is time to rationalize the product line, and reduce the number of SKUs where possible.

Ecosystem. Your ecosystem extends beyond your linear value chain to include networks and partnerships. Apple's ecosystem includes scads of software developers who create iPhone apps. This is a time to question whether you have the right partners. Are they financially and competitively stable? Are there ways to expand your relationship that benefits both you and them? Are there others you would like to partner with? Healthy players may be eager to realign their own relationships in favor of other financially sound companies.

Geographic footprint. As you look at where you sell, produce, source, and hire, geopolitics should play a role. So should exchange rates. As Indorama Ventures CEO and CFO DK Agarwal notes, "For many countries, you must have hedges to protect against currency issues. You can't be naked, because you're using cash. Robust risk management, like for foreign exchange and credit risk, is vital when you operate in many emerging countries, as we do, in the present volatile market."

"If you're doing segmentation, you should also be looking at the world by region," says Raj Ratnakar of DuPont. "For example, the change in India's inflation rates may be no different than before, while some other countries may have a lower inflation outlook. Do you want to have more exposure to that part of the world?"

Look at how earnings growth will vary. You will probably want to put more emphasis on where there will be more stability and more sustainability of cash growth. Look at where the markets are going and how you are positioning for the long term.

Portfolio mix. If you have a portfolio of businesses and are considering merging, acquiring, or divesting, think about how they will fare in inflation. Ratnakar says, "If you believe you're going into a sustainably high-inflation world for the next ten years, then you have to make choices around that. It becomes a tool in your portfolio toolkit of where to play or not to play, which businesses you want to sell, and which business you want to buy into."

Deploying capital always forces a choice. With a rising and changeable cost of capital and a strain on cash, the choices are different.

"In M&A, we look at how markets are going, where we want to be long term, and where our position is evolving relative to macro changes around the world," Ratnakar explains. "Deciding where to deploy capital and where to retrench is ongoing. It's based on a view of the portfolio strategy three years out minimum, which regions are more interesting, and which types of businesses are interesting and might actually change."

Does the cost of capital make a difference? "The cost of capital definitely impacts decisions regardless of what return metric you use—IRR, ROIC, NPV, or another," Ratnakar says. "When the cost of capital was low, it was easier to pay a higher multiple for faster-growing companies. If interest rates double or triple in short order, companies will be more careful in the multiples they can afford for assets. If the valuations of high-growth companies fall in proportion to the cost of capital, then there is no change in our strategy, but if assets are mispriced for long, we might lean more on businesses with slightly lower yet accretive growth that generate higher levels of cash."

THE NECESSITY OF INNOVATION

Innovation is a must. Whether you're in a steady economy or an inflationary one, facing recession or stagflation, you have to keep searching for how you can serve the customer better. In the face of rising costs, innovation is how you can justify a higher price. "If you just keep increasing the price for the same products," Ratnakar says, "at some point customers won't like you, or someone else will outsmart you."

You may have to do some triage to protect the most important innovation projects based partly on your cash-generation needs. Pick some initiatives you can execute quickly so you reap benefits in the near term. Be realistic as you map out the timing of the cash the project will consume and the cash it is expected to generate. Do the same for long-term projects. Fund those that still show promise in the new economic conditions.

The higher cost of capital and strain on cash raises the stakes for making the right choices, and you should bring multiple perspectives to bear on those decisions. Sales reps, the marketing team, and customers themselves should be part of the information gathering, if not the decision making—not just R&D. Customers can be great partners in guiding which features or redesigns matter to them.

THE NECESSITY OF DIGITALIZATION

You might sense that your resources are dwindling under inflation, but there's one way to stop the trend: digitalize at least some aspects of your business. You might think the time is wrong for such a huge financial drain, but that belief is flawed in several ways.

Digitalization does not have to be an all-at-once project that takes many years and lots of money to complete. Many applications are available at relatively low cost and can be implemented in months, not years. When used to address a critical pain point in the business, one single short-term project can help you survive inflation or recession. It can free up cash and/or increase revenues and margins, providing funding for the next improvement.

Digitalization is simply too fundamental to your competitiveness to be delayed. It can transform your very business model. Companies like Amazon, Netflix, and Facebook have shown that the more you digitalize your product or service, the more you increase your cash gross margin. That's because of the law of increasing returns. That is, when much of the product or service is digitalized, as it is for things like software and video-streaming services, the cost of selling each additional unit is very small, even approaching zero. Gross margin increases exponentially, and the company becomes a cash-generation machine. What's more, technology allows the company to customize its recommendations and offerings for individual consumers, so customer value increases in lockstep with shareholder value.

Algorithms will help you segment markets on the micro level and more accurately predict demand. They can synthesize information in real time so you can respond sooner.

"Things are changing so fast as we transition from a period of low inflation to higher inflation," Ratnakar says. "In the past, an analyst could spend three or four days putting data into a nice report, and we were happy with that. But now, when you have to look at data much more frequently, it's not possible to have an analyst crunch the numbers. Therefore, we have invested significantly in digital tools that dynamically show us current operating metrics like current raw-material and freight pricing, sometimes updated to the day, or live market prices, all of which feeds into our operating decisions."

An agriculture company reducing waste from inaccurate forecasts of demand, a tech company getting innovations to market faster, a bank pinpointing which prospects are likely to become new clients—these are the kinds of things that will help you reduce cost and ease cash. All of them can be digitalized.

Family businesses or those owned by private equity might take this economic period as a chance to pull ahead because they can be less concerned about a temporary dip in earnings. They can keep prices the same, thereby increasing consumer trust, and fund innovation and a digitalization project. The message for everyone else is to manage costs and pricing well enough to fund some digitalization and keep investors informed about why you're doing what you're doing: to sustain the company amid rising costs and build enduring shareholder value.

HOW TVS MOTORS ADAPTED ITS BUSINESS MODEL

TVS Motors, based in Bengaluru, India, had a thriving business selling two- and three-wheel motor bikes in a vibrant industry for many years, deriving about 40% of its revenue from overseas. When costs started to rise and demand in certain markets began to slide, the company was not quite ready for the change. Like many Indian companies operating largely in emerging markets, it had grown accustomed to a robust pace of industry growth.

But in early 2022, Managing Director Sudarshan Venu and his team were spurred into action. "To put it candidly, we were not organized around planning for inflation when costs started to rise," he told us. "We were focused, as always, on cost reduction, but then I read a paper Ram had written on inflation, and after that I spent several days reading more. I knew we had to do more than just doubling down on cost reduction."

Efforts to stay ahead of inflation ultimately led to significant changes in the customer mix and the moneymaking formula. Those changes led to a new business model that is allowing TVS Motors to ride the wave of inflation rather than succumb to it.

Segmenting and Innovating for Customers. When Venu saw a limit to the additional costs that could be passed to the consumer through pricing, he began to look at the market more granularly. Where did TVS Motors have pricing power so it could take a more aggressive stance on pricing? Who were the customers that were no longer profitable to serve?

The mass market was shrinking, and multiple competitors were vying for their share of it. Excess capacity in the industry would surely weaken pricing power further, even as costs continued to increase, pushing that market into a recession or stagflation scenario.

It made sense, then, to focus on a smaller, more profitable segment.

Venu saw that many customers still had the resources and willingness to pay for products with exciting features, and TVS Motors had an inherent capability to produce them. Serving those customers well would require the company to continue doing what it had always done—innovate—but with inflation factored in.

"Even when we were doing cost reduction, we did not cut innovation," Venu says, "because innovation is a core part of our culture and something my father has emphasized since the company's inception. We could channel it to launch more premium products and charge appropriately for them.

"However, we had to get the balance right. Everyone remembers paying the same price for a smaller candy bar, but that is something we wanted to avoid. We want to develop the features customers want and will pay for. Where we may have over-featured a product and we're not getting the pricing, we have to manage the balance and focus on what the customers really want."

Focusing product development on a more profitable segment promised to boost margins, which would allow TVS Motors to launch more premium variants. Some features could also be used to differentiate entry-level products.

Under inflation, the speed of product development also became more important. Concerns that costs would continue to rise put pressure on R&D to finish and release new products sooner, which reduced the lag in introducing an innovation and meant cash would come in sooner as well.

Changing the Dealer Network. After Venu pondered which customers were no longer profitable to serve, he circled back to the dealers that sold TVS's motorbikes. Two years earlier, he and his team had analyzed the dealers and made a startling discovery. "We used to give credit to dealers, but we found that supply chain lending was not the best use of our capital," Venu says.

"With a variety of banks so flush with liquidity, they were able to outcompete us in some segments. Hence, we made a change. We stopped extending credit to dealers and switched to cash and carry. With proper planning, that call two years ago turned out to be outstanding. We supported the dealers in arranging their own financing and helped them by working closely with banks and financial institutions."

The change exposed some weaknesses in the supply chain. It encouraged skin-in-the-game for the dealers and incentivized them to make sure they carried enough product to make as many sales as they could. It set the stage for higher velocity. "To get financing, they had to get their balance sheets in order, and now with inflation they have to manage their costs," Venu says. "Fixing those gaps will help the whole value chain cope with inflation."

The Business Model in Motion. The combined changes in customer mix, product mix, product development, value chain, and moneymaking are working together to help TVS Motors weather inflation and the already present slowdown in the mass market for motorbikes. Whereas some companies are likely to wash out, TVS Motors found ways to increase its margins and build financial strength—for itself, and for the whole value chain.

"Now we have accelerated our innovation process and are launching some new products that are in good demand," Venu explains. "Because the dealer network is more efficient, we can get those products to the consumer faster. Hence, our market share has been growing steadily."

TVS Motors has been growing faster than the market, and its market share is at an all-time high. Their brand image has also become more premium.

Venu further adds, "The dealers benefit by having products that are in demand and become financially prudent. We don't finance their stock; they pay cash on delivery, so the sales channel is fully geared to deal with inflation."

Microsegmentation of products, customers, and dealers, combined with innovation of premium products that can command higher pricing, has created a healthier company, albeit with a smaller share of the mass market. This positions the company for high profitable growth when inflation subsides because TVS Motors will have reduced waste, become more focused, accelerated product development, and enhanced its brand.

TVS will also emerge with capabilities it didn't have before—positive cash flow that can fund algorithms, data analytics that will improve microsegmentation, and the innovation process itself. That's where Venu's sights are set: "We are looking to use structured data in a more scientific way to guide which customers to serve, what products they want, and where we can conserve," he says.

Inflation Is Everybody's Business: Your Role

Armed with a general understanding of how inflation affects a business, you are better prepared to help your company succeed despite it. But that is not enough. Every business function has a role to play in coping with inflation and preparing for what will follow. Actions you take now will not only mitigate the damage from inflation but also strengthen the company so it will be well positioned when the economy takes a turn for the better. This chapter is a series of short sections to help you zero in on how your particular job or function can make a material difference:

- For the CEO
- For the CFO and Finance
- For Sales and Marketing
- For Operations

- For Procurement
- For the CIO and IT Department
- For Research and Development
- For Public Relations and Investor Relations
- For Human Resources
- For the Board

FOR THE CEO

A CEO has two broad mandates: leader of the business and leader of its people. Of course they are intertwined, but under inflation, recession, or stagflation, neglecting either one of these responsibilities is high risk. If you're not a CEO but lead a business unit or division, many of these lessons will also apply to you.

As trustee of the business, the CEO has four critical areas to focus on:

1. **Cash coming in, going out, and its timing.** Chapter three explained why working capital, capital expenditures, and debt are so touchy now; they are the cause of many company failures in earlier periods of high inflation. The CEO should work with the CFO to set up alerts and do planning on a cash basis. Every major

financial decision must be viewed through the lens of cash.

2. **Pricing, and making it happen.** It is a specialized expertise that requires analytics, but it cannot be fully delegated. The CEO must understand the basic choices in philosophy and tactics to ensure that the company is doing well for both itself and its customers. He or she will have to be hands-on with sales and marketing to be sure they are moving fast and smart on pricing. It may be necessary to reassign some leaders if they are unable to implement price changes. The company simply can't afford to wait for leaders to catch up. To protect real profitability, you'll need to revisit key contracts and change those that lock you into a situation that could lead to a cash shortage. As CEO, you may have to be personally involved in managing long-term contracts for inflation, especially those with key customers. It demands courage.

3. **The business model and strategy.** The focus on cash and pricing is likely to drive some changes in the mix of customers and segments served. The focus of the business may change to conserve cash or to pounce on opportunities that open up because competitors have slipped. No matter what, you must continue to build the future even as you focus intensely on the day-to-day immediacies.

4. **Operations.** Linking with the chief operating officer keeps a CEO grounded in how costs are changing, supply and demand are matching up, and problems are being addressed. In a manufacturing company, the COO is in charge of the bulk of the work force and is therefore first to know about issues with talent and wages. The COO's perspective will inform communications with the investment community.

Those four items alone will not sustain the business. In this time of pronounced economic volatility, the CEO must also be the chief integrator of people and information. This role involves psychological leadership, helping others to face reality and adapt their behavior. But it also has a mechanical component, which includes establishing a war-room-type mechanism and a cadence of frequent communication.

When it comes to psychology, start with your own. In good times, you were probably aggressive and optimistic in your pursuit of profits, EPS, or EBIDTA. But don't forget the balance sheet—working capital, cash, financing, and refinancing. Be aware that inflation creates the illusion of growth when revenue dollars increase for the same number of units sold.

You have to be judicious about capital allocation and therefore may need to scale back plans to gain market share. Scaling back, slowing growth, giving up cash-draining segments or customers—all of this may feel unnatural. It may even feel risky, given that you have likely built your career on growth and were compensated for it. This is the psychological shift you have to make before you can truly lead others.

Be a leader of people who pulls the organization together. Take others along the path with you. Much of a company's daily work takes place in vertical silos, dispersed geographies, and small teams, some of which meet virtually. The flow of information and ideas into and out of these pockets can be slow—too slow to adapt to abrupt changes in the economy.

Create mechanisms for information to flow, digitally or through meetings you personally take hold of. When you bring people together, how you conduct the dialogue is as important as the content. You will get better solutions and faster alignment if you keep the following goals in mind:

- Bring relevant information and ideas to the surface

- Generate alternatives

- Listen and build on good ideas

- Draw out and resolve any conflicts

- Model the openness to change and pace of action that is now required.

Inflation has stirred up a lot of anxiety and insecurity. Communication directly from you will help calm people's emotions. You have to instill a sense of urgency, but also convey confidence that changes can be made and solutions can be found.

You could start by saying, "We're going to win in this new environment," and follow up with some specifics about how. Be candid. If you're going to take some costs out and change some KPIs (key performance indicators), say so—no filtering, no hiding bad news. Assure employees that you are not just making shoot-from-the-hip decisions and that there is a plan to move forward.

Make information accessible to people through a website or dashboard that is updated often, and educate employees by including short bits of news such as Federal Reserve policy statements and government data.

YOUR CHECKLIST

- ☐ Shift your psychology from high growth
- ☐ Watch the balance sheet
- ☐ Rethink the business model and capital investments
- ☐ Pull people together with open, honest, and frequent communication

FOR THE CFO & FINANCE

Inflation has turned the CFO's world upside down. The pressure on cash touches every part of the business, so CFOs must be actively involved with virtually every business function. They have to be the visible hand pushing for changes in pricing, contract terms, and inventory levels while revisiting assumptions embedded in formal allocation processes and rules of thumb. Above all, they must be sure management has a clear picture of the company's cash situation on a daily basis.

The CFO should be keenly aware of the cash traps described in chapter two and have financial analysts work with others in the company to find the right levels of inventory to balance customer demand and cash needs. He or she may have to be the mediator between manufacturing and purchasing and sales and marketing.

Finance also needs to take a stronger role in managing accounts receivables. Collection is generally delegated to a small department in the finance department staffed by people with limited scope. Given the likelihood that receivables will become a major cash trap, it might be wise to put a high-caliber analyst in charge of receivables, and have the person report directly to the CFO.

Pricing is now critical to sustaining the company in the near term (think cash flow) and in the longer term (retaining customers). Financial analytics must be part of the decision-making about pricing and contract terms. CFOs should put someone in finance in charge of pricing analytics and connect that person with marketing and sales. Together they can assess the true profitability and cash drains of individual customers, as well as their financial stability and risk of default.

The finance department should also support leaders in updating financial assumptions and reevaluating budgets and capital expenditures, even those that have already been approved. At budget time, watch for leaders whose projections are overly optimistic or backward looking.

As CFO, the more you communicate, the greater your impact will be. Your ability to provide factual information about where the company stands, what is at risk, and what people can actually do to help keep the company on solid ground will build on the CEO's efforts and help direct people's energy toward the common goal.

Communication must also extend to the investment community, which is hungry for guidance about the company's short- and long-term prospects at a time when projections are hard to make. According to investor and governance advisory firm PJT Camberview, guidance has ebbed in periods of uncertainty but is currently flowing: whereas about 40% of S&P companies withdrew guidance at the start of the pandemic, some 95% of S&P companies issued guidance in the first quarter of 2022.

Investors want to know: How is the company navigating inflation and preparing for a possible recession or stagflation? What assumptions are your projections based on? Choose metrics that are consistent over time, and be sure the qualitative commentary is based on realism, including inflation's cumulative effect.

YOUR CHECKLIST

- ☐ Watch for cash traps
- ☐ Take charge of working capital
- ☐ Check the assumptions in planning and capital expenditures
- ☐ Communicate with investors

FOR SALES AND MARKETING

Sales and marketing should reread the chapter on pricing and take it to heart. Missing the timing and magnitude of price changes is a risk to cash and can set the company far behind others financially, eventually crippling its ability to compete. Because pricing is so critical, the sales force cannot be left to its own devices in setting prices. It must use the analytics finance can provide by sector and by individual customer to know the true profitability of each account, and grasp the urgency management conveys. That could be the difference between the company staying above water or not.

Sales and marketing executives should know their options and be open to creating an entirely new approach to pricing. Do the work of segmentation, getting outside help if you need it.

Muster the courage to implement necessary price changes, even if you're the first, and use the power of logic, encouragement, and incentives to drive the sales force to keep conversations with customers going.

Data are your friend, so be sure you are getting timely information from your salespeople on what customers are thinking, especially about the competition. Explore what your IT department can do to help gather competitive information. For example, scraping websites. The idea is not to simply follow what others are doing.

Training sessions can help prepare people in marketing and sales to operate in this new environment. For example, one retail company Ram worked with was having a difficult time increasing prices for Walmart, one of its biggest customers. So, it got a former Walmart executive to come and role-play with the team. Hearing directly from people elsewhere in the company who have succeeded in getting customers to accept price increases can also reduce the fear.

YOUR CHECKLIST

☐ Work on segmentation and customer profitability

☐ Update the pricing approach

☐ Ask IT to help with competitive data

☐ Train for the new customer dynamic

FOR OPERATIONS

In manufacturing companies, operations has taken center stage in fighting inflation but usually with a mandate that is narrower than it should be. As senior leaders see raw material and energy costs zooming, they seek to maintain margins by squeezing every bit of savings from the production process itself.

A smart operations team will get ahead of the curve in finding those opportunities to conserve costs and spending. Balram Mehta, COO at ReNew Power, gave an example of how his operations group helps deal with inflation: "If borrowing costs skyrocket, they can judge where it makes sense to turn Capex (replacing equipment) into Opex (fixing the existing equipment). Or they might see that converting to more efficient machinery is the better route to generating cash, especially as the effects of inflation accumulate."

One investment that operations might advocate is for additional applications of technology. Few sizable plants are starting from scratch when it comes to digital technology, but the rise of small third-party software vendors has opened vast opportunities to increase the use of digitalization at relatively low cost with short payback periods. As ReNew's Mehta says, "From my experience, everything in operations is easy to manage with digitalization—from determining optimal inventory levels and optimal resource utilization to removing and fixing bottlenecks and managing inventory."

Modern production teams are geared to making small improvements, and those incremental improvements in multiple areas add up. Mehta continues, "While the CEO and CFO are focused on bigger expenses, operations can look at a dashboard of 50 or 60 items on a daily basis and manage them daily. The operations team knows the issues, and they know the solution. When everything is on a dashboard, their action is very fast."

Operations will have important insights into which assets to shed or shut down. They should take the initiative to articulate them. Shape options under scenarios of varying degrees of financial stress and share them with top management.

Keeping communication flowing with the CEO is important for two additional reasons. One is to keep the CEO informed about how the work force is reacting to changes caused by inflation. In manufacturing companies, operations has the most direct relationship with the vast majority of employees through daily supervision of their work. It will know what is happening with wages, rewards, and morale in general.

The second reason is to keep employees up to date on the company's issues and direction. Says Mehta, "This is a way of boosting motivation by saying, yes, inflation is an important issue, but we all have to face it. And we can."

Operations' point of view and plans will be useful to sales and marketing as well. Mehta has found that his team has great credibility with customers and can be a great support to the sales force.

Take that credibility to the investment community. The operations team should tell the investor relations team everything it has done and is preparing to do to deal with inflation.

YOUR CHECKLIST

☐ Revisit and recommend Capex versus Opex

☐ Use digital applications to keep improving

☐ Be a conduit between front-line employees and management

☐ Help investor relations build credibility

FOR PROCUREMENT

In ordinary times, procurement, or purchasing, is considered a narrow job and not as important as many other business functions. It's expected to buy the right amount of the right product at a price that is discounted by at least as much as the company's biggest competitors get. Now, rising costs and shortages of critical resources give purchasing executives a bigger role.

They still have to hold the line on cost wherever they can, but they also have to ensure the continuity of supply. That's not easy when there's uncertainty, not just about when the materials will arrive and what the cost will be, but also exactly *what* will be in short supply. As one CEO told us, "However bad we think shortages of critical materials might be, it could get even worse. Some of our suppliers use materials from Ukraine or Russia—whether it's titanium, molybdenum, or potash—and we don't know how they will be affected. We are trying to assess what actions might occur that would affect the second-, third-, or fourth-tier suppliers we depend on."

Purchasing people need to work as partners with vendors, gather as much information as they can, and share that intelligence with people who need to know. Product development, for example, will want a heads-up that they need to search for alternative designs or formulas, marketing may need to hike prices, and sales should know not to sell what the company can't produce.

Purchasing also needs a quicker pace to lock in supply and prices as soon as possible. The chief procurement officer might want to work with the CEO to streamline decision making to allow for faster approvals.

YOUR CHECKLIST

- ☐ Secure supply
- ☐ Gather intelligence
- ☐ Keep management informed
- ☐ Be decisive

FOR THE CIO AND IT DEPARTMENT

However deeply mired you may be in multiyear digitalization projects and keeping the existing systems up and running, you now have to lift your horizon and refocus. The business will need digital capability to fight inflation on multiple fronts, squeeze out costs across the value chain, boost efficiency in production, analyze customer data, apply dynamic pricing, and keep key moneymaking metrics front and center. The company's ability to react quickly depends critically on the real-time data and analytics only digitalization can provide.

You will have to work with management to reset your priorities and deliver projects that will generate cash in a short period of time. If you have been focused on a "big bang" approach to digitalization, you might not realize that other options might be better right now. In recent years, a cottage industry of third-party vendors has arisen to build and implement targeted digital applications. These vendors can work with you to implement a project in months, not years, at a cost more like $400,000 than $4 million.

Chances are that your internal IT people are simply not equipped to do bite-sized projects that can deliver results so quickly. This is a critical time to learn about best practices outside your company and enlist help. You can read about or reach out to other companies that have solved specific problems. Larsen & Toubro, for example, freed up cash by using digital tools to manage accounts receivables. Li & Fung freed up cash-trapped inventory by using digital tools to better match supply and demand.

The benefits of digitalization are rarely in dispute. The fact that digitalization was a huge differentiator in the COVID-19 pandemic has removed the doubt. For obvious reasons, retailers that had established e-commerce capabilities far surpassed those that were almost exclusively brick and mortar.

It comes down to money. In the context of rising costs, every capital expenditure and operating expense will be scrutinized. The CEO may be reluctant to undertake a new

IT project if others aren't finished. Take a new approach and take charge. The digital vendors we know of will help make your case with deliverables and paybacks that are only months away and can help fund the next small project.

YOUR CHECKLIST

☐ Learn the new business priorities

☐ Do small projects with a short-term payoff

☐ Find ways to help business leaders

☐ Use outside help for low cost and speed

FOR RESEARCH AND DEVELOPMENT

R&D cannot be walled off from the pressures of inflation. A fresh look at the allocation of total R&D resources, going forward three to five years, is the first step in adjusting to the new environment.

Long-term "blue sky" projects may be considered sacrosanct because they represent the company's future, but short-term innovation efforts will sustain the business in the face of rising costs. Long-term projects may promise big breakthroughs, but incremental improvements to products and processes will provide value to customers and justify higher prices.

Tight resources force hard choices. Cutting or downsizing a project means losing the potential breakthrough and also the talent that worked on it. Even if the project continues, if wages fall behind competitors, you will lose good people.

In consultation with the CEO and CFO, R&D leaders must decide which resources and projects are to be preserved and which should be jettisoned. Remaining projects should be rank-ordered in terms of importance to the company in the post-inflation, post-recession world.

R&D leaders can seek other ways to tap resources—for example, by partnering with other companies on some projects and reassigning the research talent that's been freed up.

Keep in mind that other companies may be facing similar constraints. You should be alert to opportunities to bring in new talent others have been forced to shed.

You can help generate resources by working closely with marketing on innovations that can be commercialized right away. You must stay up to date on how customer needs and priorities are changing. Identify precisely what incremental changes customers would value and work on those.

This is a time to rein in the bells and whistles in favor of carefully targeted features and price points. Use new technologies to change product attributes or processes.

YOUR CHECKLIST

☐ Step up short-term projects

☐ Work to retain talent for the long term

☐ Use resources creatively

☐ Keep up with what customers value now

FOR PUBLIC RELATIONS AND INVESTOR RELATIONS

All the questions about the timing and severity of inflation and recession have created anxiety internally as well as externally. The communications staff should reach out to national and local media to demonstrate that the company is solid, methodical, and has a realistic view of the environment. Comms should be prepared to demystify the company's situation and plans for reporters and editors.

That means educating yourself first on what is happening on the macroeconomic front and in the industry, then spending time with senior leaders to gather relevant current information. Whatever information you convey must be specific and accurate, or you will quickly lose credibility with unnerved investors.

You have to be prepared to explain what many will be wondering about: What is the company's current view of the economy, and how is it working through these challenges?

Investor relations will face those questions and more. If that's your role, you must learn in detail from the CFO and others how the company's performance indicators will be affected by inflation and an economic slowdown. Balram Mehta, COO at Renew, recommends also spending time with the people in operations, and maybe even putting them in direct communication with investors because they generally have high credibility.

Although sales will have to deal directly with customers when it comes to raising prices, those changes won't happen in a vacuum. Investors will want to understand the company's rationale. How will those price changes affect market share, growth, and therefore stock valuations? There's a lot of fear that market share will take a hit and competitors will surge ahead. Talk to people in sales and marketing so you can provide examples of where the company has made price changes and what the impact was or is expected to be.

Spend the bulk of your time with the buy side, and learn from it. What does it see happening in the industry? What are other companies doing about pricing? Pay attention to their behavior. For example, watch or ask what subsectors investors are moving toward. That will tell you how inflation is playing out across the industry and the economy. Be sure to share that information internally, as it may be an early warning signal.

Some IR heads and their CEOs make a point of talking with critical investors to probe their assumptions about the economy and the industry. They ask for their views, then say, "I'd like to share our view of the industry under inflation."

Creating a dialogue with people on the buy side is the most important thing an IR person can do to help the company. It's also important to seek out big investors who are likely to grasp and support the company's positioning and prospects in the post-inflation world.

YOUR CHECKLIST

- ☐ Know how your company fits in the macro environment
- ☐ Be clear about the company's plans and actions
- ☐ Be ready to explain big pricing moves
- ☐ Learn what investors are thinking and doing

FOR HUMAN RESOURCES

Now that we've broken from the longstanding pattern of economic stability, HR should help reassess whether the people in leadership roles are up to the challenge. Leaders must fully understand the nature of the environment we are in and be willing to make the necessary shifts in psychology and habits. Can they take the offensive? Adopt flexible strategies and tactics? Sacrifice resources and preapproved plans for the sake of the company's overall situation?

Ram has said many times that 2% of the people in a company have 98% of the impact. If you get the 2% right, they will build the rest. The CHRO should work with the CEO to identify the people in critical leadership roles, then overcommunicate with those people so they all understand how the world is changing, the centrality of cash, how the goals are changing, and so on.

The hard truth is that some leaders may be unsuited to the current demands of the job. HR can help identify those who are struggling and, on the flip side, the up-and-coming leaders who may be able to step up. One senior executive told us, "We have changed leaders in a number of places, some of them exactly because they're unable to implement the changes we needed to make. They failed at it, and we can't afford to sit and wait for them to catch up. Our P&L was getting devastated."

Every company will want to lower its costs, and reducing headcount may come into play at some point. You should ensure that things are done properly. If the media senses that the company is struggling, you might find competitors trying to lure your talent. Treating people with dignity and honesty, even under tense circumstances, is essential to reduce anxiety and retain talent.

You can help reduce people's anxiety by helping them understand how inflation and an economic slowdown will affect the business. Use HR's training resources to design programs that explain how the economic realities are affecting your company and what various functions can do in response. Learning about the importance of pricing to protect cash flow, for example, can really open people's eyes. Those programs, best taught by the company's own executives, will go far in reassuring people that the company will survive and thrive.

Roberto Bettini, former group head of HR for Indorama Ventures, had his group conduct training sessions tailored to various business functions, such as sourcing and sales. "For example, we prepared the sales force to negotiate contracts on a range of elements such as service levels, quality, and partnership to avoid focusing on price alone. Don't fall into that trap!"

Help update KPIs. Chances are they are now misaligned. Changing them soon is important because they do guide behavior. HR must ensure that people have clarity about any revised goals and incentives. In a noninflationary environment, compensation typically is based on a single metric: bottom-line results, usually stated as operating profit. In inflationary times, cash is critical, and incentives should reflect that. Compensation formulas really should have a minimum of four indicators: such as cash, operating profit, working capital, and customer satisfaction.

Managers may object to changing the compensation plan, but if you enlist their help in crafting it, they are more likely to buy in. Whether or not that happens, you have to be sure the plan is executed fairly.

Inflation will almost surely distort measures of performance in the short term, so work quickly to distinguish between numbers that look better than they are because of inflation. It might appear that someone has grown his or her unit because revenue dollars have increased, but was more product sold? Work with the CFO to ensure that performance is evaluated on real numbers, not inflated numbers. When units are competing for resources, rewarding the wrong thing causes talent to walk away.

One more thing on HR's plate: if the business has to make fundamental changes in geography or business model in response to inflation and/or a slowdown, HR has to adjust the skills mix accordingly. You may have the opportunity to grab talent from companies that are not adjusting well.

The board should know what HR is doing to protect talent, given its importance to any company. Offer to do a presentation for the board to show how you intend to lead HR under inflation, recession, or stagflation. The board will respect you for it.

YOUR CHECKLIST

- ☐ Help identify those who can't adapt
- ☐ Defend fair treatment in times of stress
- ☐ Keep KPIs up to date
- ☐ Use training to build skills and reduce anxiety

FOR THE BOARD

In good times, directors tend to give the CEO a lot of leeway within the outline of an overall strategy the board has approved. Most try not to overstep into micromanaging the business. But in this period, the board has to step up to make sure that management is moving quickly and radically enough to fend off serious damage from inflation and/or recession.

If your CEO has not sprung to action yet, take charge and set the pace. Ask for a meeting right away devoted solely to a discussion of how inflation and recession will affect the company, or propose an off-site where management can present plans under various scenarios. That session could include outside experts who lay out the emerging risks or leaders of other businesses who can discuss how they navigated inflation.

Cash traps can form quickly, so don't just assume the CEO is taking preemptive steps. You need to know how management is handling cash and capital allocation. Even if you haven't lived through periods of high inflation yourself, as a director you can be a great coach by asking thoughtful questions, such as these:

- If the inflation rate goes from X to Y, how will that affect working capital?

- What are the three greatest risks to our liquidity?

- What application of digital technology could help us

generate more cash in the next six to nine months?

- What do we need to withdraw funds from?

- What would make your business model obsolete?

Speed matters, so if the top team is not prepared to answer these questions, encourage it to get help with the analysis. Outsiders can be a useful check on whether the proposed scenarios are realistic or wide-ranging enough.

The board also needs to have its own sense of urgency on a couple of fronts. The most critical issue is revising the goals and compensation incentives one to two years out for the new context so they are driving the right behaviors. Most boards have already made a big mistake by not setting a cash goal for management. In an inflationary environment, EPS or EBITDA alone can get the company in trouble. Before approving goals and plans that are two or three years forward, be sure the projections take the cumulative effects of inflation into account.

A dashboard can help the board keep closer watch on financial developments. This is crucial for cash-strapped companies in low-margin businesses, and doubly so if such companies have high debt with restrictive covenants.

The board must also be attuned to qualitative factors, such as management's sense of urgency. If the CEO and top team appear to be lagging for some reason, directors have to wake them up. It's one thing to learn about the importance of price changes, for example, but is the CEO or head of sales too slow to implement them? Maybe these people fear the loss of market share. Maybe they need help working with a large customer. When the board sees blockages to implementation, it should help overcome them.

The more robust the analysis of inflation's effects, the better. Directors should encourage management to delve deeply and think broadly about inflation's effects. How will inflation affect the entirety of the company's value chain and what is the plan to contend with those impacts? No two companies will be impacted in exactly the same way. It's important to understand how every part of the ecosystem will be affected. How will different sectors of the economy fare? Clearly some will be hit harder than others. Where do we stand?

Capital spending will almost certainly be constrained. Directors should work with management to create a new framework for allocating resources. That includes reallocation, meaning withdrawing money from one initiative and redirecting it to a more important one. Shareholders will still expect the company to be moving forward on things like sustainability, and the board has to protect those interests. Directors need to help the CEO make trade-offs, then be sure the reallocations are aggressive enough to keep pace with the realities of moneymaking.

The board's compensation committee has the important but complex task of deciding how to compensate the CEO and senior management in the context of slower growth and the changing real value of a dollar. The typical senior executive's three-to-five-year compensation plan—which is usually 25% fixed and 75% variable—is a sacred cow that should be killed off in favor of a more realistic plan.

The compensation committee must look at the company's financial statements not only in nominal dollars but also in real dollars adjusted for inflation. Only real-dollar comparisons will tell you the actual economic value that management created or destroyed.

Quantitative goals are hard to set in uncertain times. Advisory firm Pay Governance saw some companies widen the performance curve or shorten the pay period to deal with uncertainty during COVID-19. The same idea applies to inflation and the risk of recession. Qualitative metrics can also be useful when the economic environment is unpredictable. Look at how these numbers were achieved—did management make the right trade-offs? What actions did the team take to reach its goals? In so doing, did it shortchange the future? A healthy discussion that includes the CEO and CFO on these topics will be useful to everyone.

As the company changes product mix, customer mix, or exits a subsector, it might realize that a new business model is needed. The board should think of strategy and business models as more fluid now, and therefore review them at least three times a year. Get updates on how the landscape is evolving, which components of the portfolio might be susceptible to significant decline, or where sudden opportunities may appear. The long-term focus is always on how to emerge stronger in the post-inflation and post-recessionary environment.

Many boards have expanded their role in recent years beyond monitoring and compliance to helping the CEO perform better. By sharing what they observe in their normal work, they can greatly enhance the company's ability to pick up early warning signals. Directors have expansive networks and geographic breadth, which give them many data points on what is happening in various sectors of the economy or various parts of the world. They may know exactly how inflation is playing out in a particular industry or country and which players are leading or lagging as a result. They may be able to detect underlying drivers that are not widely recognized. These inputs can save the CEO by giving him or her a clearer picture of what is happening in the macro environment in time to reposition the business and prepare for opportunities that emerge. A better reading of early warning signals can be a game changer.

YOUR CHECKLIST

☐ Spur management to action

☐ Help break bottlenecks

☐ Use a framework for capital allocation

☐ Revise the compensation plan

Ram's Closing Message

I hope you now feel prepared to lead. It is leaders who let companies decline or take them to new heights. This could be your time to shine.

The things that will help you lead through inflation will also help you lead when the next change comes. Use the external change to your advantage, and get everyone aboard to navigate through the rough patch. Take the hand you are dealt. Use it to create new value for the customer, shareholders, and the other constituencies you serve. That's how you and your company will come out ahead and be ready to ride high when stability and growth return—as we know they will.

Acknowledgments

We have had the extreme privilege of learning from some of the best business leaders in the world as they coped with inflation in real time. We are especially grateful to DK Agarwal, Roberto Bettini, Dennis Carey, Albert Chao, James Chao, John Chao, John Chiminski, Dave Flitman, David Kohler, Harsh Mariwala, Balram Mehta, Raj Ratnakar, and Sudarshan Venu for sharing their time, thoughts, and experiences. Their candor in describing the challenges they faced makes this book a far more valuable teaching tool, and their leadership is clearly something to emulate.

Adam Echter took time with us to dive into the intricacies of pricing, a critical area in inflation. His and his colleagues' collective experience in this area was a great gift to us and to our readers.

Before we rushed to create a practical guidebook for dealing with inflation, we produced an article for *Chief Executive* magazine. Dan Bigman, editor and chief content officer for Chief Executive Group, got the ball rolling for the article and for subsequent teaching sessions on the topic. But Dan insisted the business community needed more. We want to thank him, Executive Chair Wayne Cooper, and CEO Marshall Cooper for their support and encouragement to go further. Thank you to Geoff Colvin and Bill Hayes for their support and input as well.

Every book is a team effort. We are grateful for all who made suggestions, helped edit, shape, produce, and coordinate: Roy Abdo, Rohit Bhargava, Cynthia Burr, Mark Fortier, Jeffrey Gantz, John Joyce, Celine Khoury, Lisa Laubert, and Sean Mathena.

A final thank you to all of the leaders who are showing resilience and optimism in fighting an enemy they've newly encountered. They are showing the way.

About the Authors

Ram Charan is a bestselling author, teacher, and world-renowned advisor to CEOs and other business leaders of some of the world's best-known companies, including: Toyota, Bank of America, Aditya Birla Group, Novartis, Fast Retailing (Uniqlo), and Humana. His work is often behind the scenes and focused on highly sensitive and fate-making issues. *Fortune* magazine published a profile of Ram in which it called him "the most influential consultant alive," and Ivan Seidenberg, former CEO of Verizon, called Ram his "secret weapon."

The author of close to forty books, four of which were bestsellers, he is known for providing real-world solutions—the kind of advice you can use Monday morning. His book *Execution*, lauded for its practicality, spent more than 150 weeks on the *New York Times* bestseller list.

Ram's energetic, interactive teaching style has won him several awards, including from GE's famous Crotonville Institute and Northwestern.

Ram was elected a Distinguished Fellow of the National Academy of Human Resources and was named one of the most influential people in corporate governance and the board room by Directorship magazine. He has served on the Blue Ribbon Commission on Corporate Governance and serves or has served on a dozen boards in the U.S., Brazil, China, India, Canada, and Dubai.

He earned an MBA with high distinction and a doctorate degree from Harvard Business School, where he was a Baker Scholar and faculty member.

Geri Willigan is an independent content developer and business writer who has worked closely with Ram Charan for nearly 30 years in a variety of roles on a broad range of projects, including bestselling books. She first crossed paths with Ram when she was an editor at *Harvard Business Review* in the late 1980s and '90s.

Geri has helped numerous preeminent experts publish classic *HBR* articles, including Michael Hammer (father of re-engineering), Stephen Roach (Yale economist), Hermann Simon (co-founder of pricing consultancy Simon-Kucher & Partners), and Fred Reichheld (Bain & Company thought leader on customer loyalty). She has also interviewed prominent business leaders, including Nike CEO Phil Knight and Disney CFO Gary Wilson.

She taught an editing course in Northeastern University's publishing program, and for many years has worked closely with Bob Buday, founder of two pioneering thought leadership consultancies: Bloom Group and Buday Thought Leadership Partners.